CW01187106

Swimming With Lead Boots

Meg Pinder

Grosvenor House
Publishing Limited

This book is published by
Grosvenor House Publishing Ltd
Link House
140 The Broadway, Tolworth, Surrey, KT6 7HT.
www.grosvenorhousepublishing.co.uk

This is a true story, but the names of the characters
have been changed to protect the privacy of those depicted.

A CIP record for this book
is available from the British Library

Paperback ISBN 978-1-83615-102-9
Hardback ISBN 978-1-83615-103-6
eBook ISBN 978-1-83615-104-3

PROLOGUE

"Never work with children or animals," so the saying goes, but my experience was that it was **not** the children or the animals that was the problem. It was other adults.

A pupil said to me one day "Miss you look like the kind of person that makes a really nice cup of tea."
That was the problem I didn't want to look like the kind of person who made a really nice cup of tea.

Come with me as I journey through thirty plus years of working as a childminder and School Support Assistant.
Laugh with me and cry with me over the most bizarre and difficult situations I found myself in.

DEDICATIONS

This book is dedicated to my tall guy.
To my beautiful girls, family, and special friends who have encouraged me and spurred me on over the past three years to complete this autobiography.

Also, to the wonderful teaching and school support staff I have worked with over the years who literally went 'above and beyond' on many occasions.
You are all amazing.

Also a special thanks to my dear friend Carole Buchan for her work on the cover design.

PART ONE

'Everyone is a genius. But if you judge a fish by its ability to climb a tree it will live its whole life believing it is stupid.'

Albert Einstein

Chapter 1

If You Can't Stand the Heat...

The sun beat down hot and hard on us, and I could taste the salty sweat on my top lip. One o'clock precisely, and there was no shade anywhere in the new playground – not one bit, nothing, zilch.

Pupils ran at speed across the sparsely filled, raised flower beds, chasing each other as kids do. But my stomach lurched, and my heart raced. One slip – that's all it would take. One slip, and I could see the boy stumble in my mind and hear the sickening sound of his head crack on the sharp edge of the wooden frame, the blood flowing down his face.

'STOP! STOP!' staff called out to the boys, but they didn't hear and carried on running.

Large, ornate mushrooms grew out of the wooden frames, much to the interest of the pupils. Concerns had been raised about the mushrooms, and a debate was ongoing about whose job it was to remove the mushrooms.

Janitors were refusing to remove them. 'Not on our remit,' they argued.

Specialists would need to be brought in to remove the mushrooms. Until then, playground staff would continue to whack them with sticks to remove them, worried that the mushrooms might end up in someone's mouth.

Once, in science class, a pupil I was supporting drank the experiment quick as a flash before either myself or the teacher could grab the beaker. Luckily, the beaker only contained salt water that day.

The heat in the playground increased minute by minute, and I could feel the sweat running down my back. A pupil ran over, snatching my sunglasses, and ran off. It was a great game; she just wanted me to chase her. But there was no time for that, as I could see a boy standing on top of another boy over on the grass.

'Hey!' I shouted. 'Get off of him.'

'Sorry, Miss,' he apologised quickly.

'It's ok, Miss,' from the boy on the grass. 'I don't mind.'

That was fine, but how would we explain to his parents the two dirty footprints on the back of his white school shirt?

From the mainstream school sharing the school campus above, a teacher shouted, and a jotter and pencil came flying out of the window and landed at my feet.

The previous Headmaster in the old school had pushed for a partial awning over our playground. He'd argued that it would give our pupils more privacy and the mainstream pupils wouldn't be able to look down on our pupils – either literally or metaphorically. It would also have given us some shade on hot days like today. His request had been denied.

Our daughter, who attended the mainstream school, confided one evening, 'Mum, we can hear you shouting in the playground. We hear weird shouts like, 'His head doesn't come off! Stop pulling!' and 'Put your clothes back on – it's wintertime!"

Her friends in class would giggle, 'That's your mum!'

But I'd had to work on that shout and find a voice that could be heard. All my life I'd felt invisible and overlooked.

It didn't help, of course, when my parents attended my first 'parents' night' at high school only to be told by 90% of the teachers that they didn't know who I was!

'Are you sure she's in this class? She obviously doesn't stand out; she's not one of the top pupils, and she's not a troublemaker.'

'Well, that was a waste of time,' my mum exclaimed on returning home. 'We won't bother doing that again.'

I was very aware of my small stature and tiny (some might say squeaky) voice.

A pupil once asked me during a full meltdown (hers, not mine), 'WHAT HAPPENED TO YOU?' She continued in an angry, accusatory tone, 'SMALL!'

I apologised for my smallness, as it seemed the most appropriate thing to do when someone was having a meltdown.

Interviews were particularly soul destroying. I could read the faces of the interviewer(s) like a book, but I became aware of this and tried to prepare well. I took time to dress to be taken seriously. I felt like I had to work hard to prove myself and overcome my 'mousy' demeanour.

When I started in the old school, I asked the Headmaster, 'Will I have to learn to shout here?'

'Not at all,' he replied. 'Consistency and fairness, that's the key. The pupils need to know that you are consistent and fair. Don't let anything go – if you let it go once, they'll do it again.'

And he was absolutely right. I learned.

A 4th year pupil constantly refused to do anything I asked. He was rude to me and even laughed in my face. I was insecure and embarrassed, my own insecurities weighing me down in this new environment. I was indeed like a fish out of water – never was a saying more appropriate. But I needed to learn how to swim... and fast!

Even with the other staff: they drank, they laughed, they partied hard. I was going to have to find a way to fit in with the staff team.

A male pupil said to me one day (obviously meaning it as a compliment), 'Miss, you look like the kind of person that makes a really nice cup of tea.'

That was the thing, though. I didn't really want to look like the kind of person that makes a really nice cup of tea!

It all came to a head one day during a rainy afternoon in the old school. A supply teacher took the class of ten boys; ten challenging boys, with different backgrounds and different abilities.

One lad from the class had zoomed in on me straight away at the beginning of term.

'I'm a murderer, Miss, did you know that? That's why I'm here.' His eyes were wide, his face in my face, looking for a reaction.

'Are you now? Is that right?' I answered, trying not to react and stay cool. 'So am I, as it happens.'

He laughed but did want to know more and wanted all the details. It was a 'spur of the moment' comment but did get me some 'street cred' from him.

I couldn't tell him that it was my girls' pet rabbit that I'd murdered... and felt awful about it for years after. I can still hear their haunting screams as they opened the cage and found poor Toffee rabbit with all four legs in the air, stiff as a board. Friends still tease me now, years later, calling me 'the rabbit murderer'.

But I mean, what are you supposed to do with a dead rabbit? Firstly, run around the kitchen in a panic, hands flapping. Secondly, call husband for advice, only to hear, 'I told you so, you're not supposed to bath rabbits.'

Lastly, find a large polybag for the rabbit until said husband comes home from work to deal with the situation. A 'Farmfoods' carrier bag, as I remember.

So, it was a rainy afternoon in the old school, and we were with the supply teacher. A teacher I'd decided was a bit 'unconventional'. A teacher who came a bit too close when he spoke to you, always with a hand on your shoulder or your arm, with an overpowering smell of cheap aftershave. A bit too 'touchy feely' for my liking!

The class played five-a-side football. But one pupil was unwilling to play, so the teacher took his place, and I sat on the bench with the pupil, making small talk, all the while dodging the ball when it came near.

These boys may have had some learning difficulties, emotional and social issues, but I couldn't fault their football skills. They knew the rules like the back of their hands.

I, on the other hand, never could work out the rules – especially the whole 'off-side' rule. I mean, what is that all about!? And what exactly is 'football intelligence'?

The room was filled with the stench of old, sweaty trainers. It was toxic! Not far off the smell of burning mouse.

I know what that smells like, as a mouse had been trapped behind a radiator in the tiny office where I worked in my first ever job. I was office junior in a company that sold tractors and farm machinery, with a workshop for repairs.

The radiator was situated right beside my desk in a small office, and as the days went on the smell was unbearable, toxic, choking. Everyone commented as they came into the office.

I didn't know what it was, but to date, I can honestly say it's the worst smell I've ever encountered.

I liked the job – my first ever job, and I was so pleased with myself to have secured a job before I even left school. Mum was delighted – and hopefully proud of me.

Secretarial Studies was my best subject at school. I loved it, and I was good at it. I do remember the teacher telling our class of 30 students one day that the chances of us actually getting a secretarial job when we left school was very slim.

'Out of this class of 30, you'll be lucky if ONE of you goes on to become a secretary. Most of you will end up in factories,' she sneered.

I was that one. And I did eventually go on to become a full-time Personal Secretary.

It wasn't easy in the wee office, though, I remember. There was just me and the Office Manager. I remember she was crazy about Elvis, so it didn't exactly earn me any Brownie points when she got on the bus one morning and sat beside me as she did every day, and I blurted out, 'So, Elvis is dead.'

She hadn't heard the news on the radio that morning, and for a moment I thought she'd stopped breathing. She looked so shocked, as if someone had slapped her, then the tears came.

It also didn't help when we had a conversation about age one day. I looked and sounded young, and I always had trouble trying to get served alcohol or get into a nightclub. I'd had to actually go to the lengths of carrying my original birth certificate around with me to prove my age. Eventually, it got very tatty and brown, ageing faster than I did.

'How old do you think I am?' she asked me that day.

She was a good bit older than me, and going by her dress sense I made an educated guess at 36. Actually, I really thought she was older than that, but I was trying to be kind.

Of course, I knew right away by the look on her face that I'd got that badly wrong. She was 26 years old – ten years older than me.

It's not easy working in an office with just one other person, as I learned over the years in different jobs.

The guys in the workshop (the bears, as they seemed to be called by the salesmen) loved the fact that they had fresh meat in the way of a new lassie in the office. They loved to tease me and send me on a 'wild goose-chase'.

'Can you phone the supplier for me, hen, and ask for another box of sky hooks?'

'Gonny ask Stuart for a long stand for me?'

That one really did confuse me, and I stood for ages waiting to be served.

There was one young 'bear' that really scared me, though. He was maybe in his twenties and a bit 'unhinged'. The other bears used to say that he was worse when it was a full moon, then they'd all laugh. Sometimes, we'd hear a lot of shouting and banging and arguing, and we knew he was 'losing it' about something.

One night I stood waiting for my bus back into the town as usual. There was only one bus per hour, so I had to time it just right if I didn't want to wait a whole hour.

Young bear pulled out of the workshop in his scarlet red sports car, raced past the bus stop, then saw me standing waiting. He stopped and reversed back.

'Hiya, wee one,' he said with that stupid sleazy grin. 'Want a lift?'

He was very unpredictable, and he scared me. So, I lied, 'No, no, it's fine. My bus will be along in a minute, I'm sure.' I'd actually missed the bus and had almost another hour to wait.

'Get in,' he urged me. 'Are you scared or something? I'm heading into town.'

I was very wary, and he could see that. His face changed, and he looked nice.

'Look, I'm heading into town anyway. I'll take you there, I promise.'

'Ok, thanks,' I agreed, and got into the tiny sports car.

As soon as I got in, his whole demeanour changed, and he raced off at top speed. He was laughing and laughing, driving so fast with a big stupid grin on his face. He reminded me of the Joker from the Batman films.

Oh God, here I was in this car with the crazy bear! My mum had warned me so many times, 'Don't get in a stranger's car. Don't go with anyone you don't know.'

But I **did** know him, didn't I? And he **wasn't** a stranger.

Oh God, oh God. Inside my head I was panicking and praying in my head, 'Let me out, let me out.'

He did drive into town, but when we reached my usual stop, he kept on driving and kept on laughing.

'Let me out,' I said in my tiny voice. Then louder, 'LET ME OUT!'

I really was panicking now. He was crazy, like the other guys had said, and he was taking me out of the town, past all the houses until we were in the countryside.

Tears welled up in my eyes and spilled out down my face. Then I was sobbing, loudly. It was an open top car, so anyone could see I was in distress.

At last he slowed down.

'Ocht, I'm just having a bit of fun with you, wee one,' he said. 'I'll take you back.' And he did take me back to town.

I never told anyone what had happened, because I felt as if I'd let myself down by accepting a lift from him. And I never accepted a lift again.

As I got out of the car that night, it was getting dark, and a full moon shone clear and bright in the sky – the face in the moon winking knowingly at me.

In the P.E. hall, the boys played on for over an hour. The teacher didn't make any attempt to call a break, and as the afternoon wore on, his behaviour changed. For a fortyish man, he was regressing into a teenage boy and becoming worryingly competitive.

I waved him over and suggested that the boys might need a break, and I would see if I could find some water bottles. From the corner of my eye I could see an argument brewing, with a bit of pushing and shoving between the boys.

'Yes, sure, go for it,' he agreed.

I went straight to the janitor's room, but there was nothing there. No water. Thankfully, I met the Headmaster in the corridor, and he pointed me in the direction of an old cupboard.

As I struggled back up the staircase with the crate of water bottles, I could hear a loud commotion coming from the P.E. hall. When I got to the door, I could see the teacher wrestling with a pupil on the floor – he had the boy in a headlock, and both of them were very red in their faces.

As I went to enter the P.E. hall, the teacher kicked the door shut with his foot, almost smacking me in the face. In the few seconds it took me to lay the crate down and turn the door handle, all hell had broken loose. The boy on the floor was crying, lying in the foetal position, and all the other boys were surrounding the teacher, everyone shouting at the same time.

The atmosphere was electric, and as a new member of staff I was scared and shaking.

'MISS, MISS, YOU SAW WHAT HAPPENED. HE PUNCHED STEVIE! THE TEACHER PUNCHED STEVIE!' the boys screamed.

But I hadn't seen what happened, because the teacher had kicked the door closed just as I got there.

From behind me I saw a shadow and turned to see the Headmaster standing, saying nothing but seeing everything. Omnipresent. He was good at that, seeing everything. He knew his kids and he knew his staff.
At three o'clock, as I was leaving the school, I passed the Headmaster's room and he called me in.
'What exactly happened up there this afternoon?' he asked quietly.
I told him what I saw, and what I hadn't seen.
That was the last time we saw the supply teacher; he never came back to the school.

The Headmaster was well respected and loved by the staff and pupils. He had a 'way' with him that almost made him 'God-like'. We would hear him whistling or singing in the corridor as he made his way around the school.
There were posters up around the school which read 'Respect is not a gift – it has to be earned'. And I think about that quote often as I travel through my life and find myself in different situations.

With the support and encouragement of the Headmaster and the Management Team, I gradually started to gain some confidence.
I spoke to the Deputy Head Teacher about the 4th Year boy.
She didn't react, but said in her quiet, calm manner, 'Walk with me.'
We made our way to the boy's class, and she quietly asked him to come out into the corridor.
'Do you know why we're here?' she asked him quietly.
The boy looked down at his shoes and shifted about awkwardly. 'Yes,' he replied.
'Why are we here?'
'Because I was rude to Miss,' he admitted.

The Deputy Head repeated what the boy had said, very slowly and deliberately.
'And how do we treat staff in this school?' she asked with an authoritative but still calm tone.
'With respect,' he said sheepishly.
'And what do we do when a member of staff asks us to do something?'
'We do it,' he replied, a red glow around his face now.
He was asked to apologise to me which he duly did.
The Deputy never raised her voice that day, or any day in all of the years we worked together. But every pupil respected her, because she was fair and consistent and respected others.
I never had any more trouble with that boy, and from then on I strived to be like the Deputy. I hoped that somehow, in time, I could learn to gain such respect from the pupils and from my colleagues.

Back in the heat of the new playground, we shaded the most vulnerable pupils with umbrellas – those in wheelchairs.
A pupil in an electric power chair scooted around the playground at speed, and staff shouted for him to slow down. But he laughed and kept going. We saw him scoot at speed up the raised incline on the grass... too late to do anything. Why we needed this artificial hill on the grass was anyone's guess!
Staff ran, but everything seemed to happen in slow motion, like a bad dream. The chair rocked unsteadily from side to side and then toppled over.
Staff came from all directions to help, but while this situation was being dealt with, another pupil took the opportunity to run. She liked to run.
A pupil shouted, 'MISS, MISS... SHE'S GONE, LOOK!

Another more able pupil had seen her go and ran after her, round the science block, into the sensory garden, and out of the gate.

'Why can't we lock those gates?' we'd asked at a staff meeting. 'We want to secure the playground. To make it safe for ALL pupils.'

'Fire regulations,' we were told.

So, the pupils ran, and they ran.

From outside the high pink fencing, the officials looked on through their rose-tinted glasses, shaking hands and congratulating themselves in designing a magnificent new building.

Chapter 2

Ace Card

So, I know about rose-tinted glasses. Oh yes, I know. Seeing the world through rose-tinted glasses, where everything looks wonderful. That maybe sounds like a good thing, but when your life is falling apart, that's when it's time to step away from the glasses.

The past has a habit of catching up with you sometimes. Sneaking up behind you without you noticing and grabbing you by the throat.

That's what happened one sunny July afternoon around 2006.

My daughter was sifting through the old photos in a tatty, old cardboard box. A box of memories, that's what it's like – all those pieces of card with memories of the past, good and bad, happy and sad.

Memories of the 'Sunday run' when we'd take grandparents out in the bulky old Standard Vanguard, with its plush, red leather seats, and the large leather armrest that pulled down from the middle of the back seat like magic and where my Barbie dolls could sit. I felt like a princess. No seat belts in the 60s, of course. Usually, we'd head north to places with funny sounding names like Auchterarder, Tomintoul, and somewhere that Mum called The Devil's Elbow, which did sound a bit scary to a five-year-old.

Mum's parents would come one week, and Dad's parents the next week. The grandparents were very different and didn't particularly get along.

I remember my dad's dad really scared me. He was tall and loud, and he'd grab me sometimes and not let go. Nana would say, 'You're frightening the bairn, Jimmy, let her go.'

The Sunday run would usually end with a stop at a fish and chip shop, and eating chips wrapped in newspaper, covered with salt and sauce. Great memories.

My daughter and I laughed at the fashions and hairstyles on the old photos.

'Who's he?' she asked.

It was a photo from the 70s, taken on a Kodak Instamatic camera. What a great thing that was at the time! Being able to get your photo right there and then out of the front of the camera, instead of the usual way of having to use all 24 photos on the spool and then handing the spool into a specialised shop to be developed.

Some spools had 36 photos on them, and it could take a year or more to use them all up. That meant that sometimes you would take the spool to the shop and wouldn't have a clue what was on it.

It could often take seven days before you got the photos printed, and of course some might not have developed properly so had nothing on them. That's why the Instamatic camera was such a great invention. But from looking through the box, it was plain to see that over the years the colours of the prints had faded greatly, and the finish hadn't worn well.

As I take a closer look of the photo, I can see a young couple, maybe about 16 or 17 years old. The same age as my daughter is now. The boy looks wild, with strong yellow hair and a rugged red complexion. He's wearing a smart tweed-effect jacket and a slim collared shirt with a skinny leather tie (all the rage in the 70s). His wild green eyes speak of Saturday night street fights.

The girl is wearing a soft brown 'coney fur' jacket, and her hair sits in blonde curls, tied back at one side with a comb clasp of soft beige coloured feathers. The girl in the photo doesn't know what 'coney fur' is, and she doesn't want to know.
Her aura of naivety is both endearing and worrying.
My daughter's eyes are on me now, watching, waiting for an answer to her question.
'He's an old boyfriend,' I tell her eventually.
'I'm glad **he's** not my dad,' she says, laughing. 'He looks scary.'
As I take the photo from her, my knees start to shake uncontrollably, and I hope my daughter doesn't notice.

Suddenly I'm back in the old flat with the white painted walls and the strong smell of new carpets. I'd spent all my savings on the flooring – brand new carpets all through the flat. But there was a flaw right up the middle of the sitting room one. The carpet fitters had been very cheeky and put a seam right up the middle, so it was never going to be right.
I've got my money box out – the box where I keep all the money my friends give me towards items they have ordered from my catalogues.
I ran three catalogues, I remember – pre-internet. Freemans, Grattan, and Littlewoods. We could order clothes, shoes, and household goods by telephone and get them delivered. Then we could pay it all up weekly.
That day there should have been over £200 in the box – a month's wages for me at the time – but the box was empty.
I ask him about the missing money, and he flies into a rage, swiping the coffee cups off the checkered, tiled mantelpiece, and sending brown coffee stains across the white walls.

And then I'm spinning and spinning around and around until I land, and my head finds something hard. Chairs and ornaments are sent crashing, and I lie still, hoping the world will stop if I close my eyes. The heavy front door slams shut, and I'm left alone.
How did this happen? How did my life become so flawed? Just like the new carpet, it was never going to be right.
From the old second-hand sideboard, the wedding invites lay laughing at me.
'7th June, 1980 – what a joke. He's never going to marry you.'
Mum never liked him, but I told her she was wrong. Time after time, she had it wrong. He just needed someone to love him, I told her.
'The eyes are the windows to the soul,' she told me, 'and I don't like what I see in his.'
We argued daily, which became exhausting. Mum trying to split us up, and me defending him and fighting to keep us together. I thought I loved him. Then I came home from work one day, and there were bags sitting at the front door.
'Just go,' she said coldly. 'Move in with him, and then you'll see what he's really like.'
It felt like I'd won. After all the arguing, I'd won, and Mum had lost the game.
But she was playing her ace card – the last card she had left in her hand.
Outside, through the heavy sash windows, there was a promise of spring. Small green shoots were poking their heads above the snow-covered soil. Usually it was my favourite time of the year, but this year was different. Something inside me, in the pit of my stomach, was slowly rotting away and dying.
Just then the sunlight shone in through the window and caught something on the old sideboard. It was his key! He'd left without his key.

I picked it up and held it tightly in my hand. I was safe as long as I held this key; he couldn't get back in.
I suppose I always knew he was a bit crazy, unpredictable, and wild. At first, it was exciting, but now it was just scary, and I couldn't go on like this. I realised it couldn't have been easy for him, living in and out of children's homes for years. And I knew he'd tried to take his own life at one point. But I couldn't go on living like this. Something had to change.
I couldn't call anyone. We'd only been in there for three weeks and there was no telephone in the flat. We were the first tenants in the newly refurbished factory flats, so there were no other neighbours to go to for help.
All night I huddled in the corner of the cold white bathroom, clutching the key, and woke to the sound of the milkman whistling in the close.
I opened my eyes and for the first time in five years they were truly open, seeing my life unravel in front of me. I couldn't and wouldn't go on living like this.
Over the years he'd dealt me card after card of hurt and pain, and now suddenly the cards were spilled out in front of me as clear as the newly-fitted windows. He was playing in clubs, while I was playing in hearts. It was time for a new hand, and this time I was dealing!

I washed and dressed for work. Through the spyhole, the painted close was silent and empty. Quietly, I opened the heavy old door and tiptoed along the shiny painted floor to the outside world, my footsteps echoing as I walked.
He was waiting just outside the entrance and grabbed me as I stepped out. A furious struggle ensued, and as we fought desperately for my bag, the strap gave way, and I was thrown onto the road in front of a car. How the driver managed to stop in time I'll never know, but I'm just glad he did.

I ran then, as fast as I could. Even in those days I couldn't run fast – later I'd be diagnosed with asthma, but back then I didn't really know why my lungs were poor.

I ran to my friendly bus driver, who was sitting at the bus terminus as he did every morning.

'Good morning, love,' he greeted me in his usual cheery manner. Then he saw the state of me, and his face changed. He got out of his seat to comfort me.

At that moment, the green-eyed monster jumped onto the bus behind me, his angry face in the bus driver's face. The driver sat back down in his seat, fearfully.

'We'll talk about this later!' he shouted in my face, his nose pressing hard against mine in a very threatening way.

When he jumped off the bus, the driver asked me quietly what I'd like to do.

'Take me to the police station,' I said shakily.

He did just that, driving silently and passing every bus stop, leaving folk frustrated and confused along the way.

The police are there to protect us. So, I reckoned I'd file a report, make a statement, and they'd help me.

Unfortunately not. The law may have changed now, but in 1980 they were unable to help me. Without any obvious signs of violence, and a lack of witnesses, there was nothing they could do.

I called his lovely mum from the red telephone box at the end of the street. When I told her I was leaving, she seemed shocked.

'No, hen, don't go. It's always sore at the time, I know, but he'll be really sorry, and you'll get a lovely bunch of flowers tomorrow.'

She knew.

She knew everything.

She'd lived like this, but I couldn't.

Her tone grew harsh then. 'I'll be wanting my butter dish back then,' she said coldly.

That's all I could offer after five years together. My sister duly delivered the thick glass butter dish.

But there was someone I could call for help. And I'm eternally grateful to my uncle and cousin and their friends who came to rescue me that evening after work. Like SAS troops, they entered the flat silently and stood over him as he slept like a baby on the furry rug in front of the gas fire. My uncle gave him a tap with his foot to wake him, and he must have got the fright of his life seeing himself surrounded by these 'larger than life' rescuers.

He didn't put up any kind of fight, I was told. Instead, he ran out of the house and left my rescuers to their task of emptying the flat of everything, including furniture and carpets.

After I left the little painted flat behind, I truly believed my life was over. I believed everything my crazy ex had told me, that no-one else would want me, I was 'used goods', unattractive. Apparently, I breathed too loud, which was one of the things that made me annoying, and one of the things that caused his anger outbursts.

All I knew as I sat in the beautiful park with the happy faces of the daffodils smiling up at me that cold, snowy day in March – my 19th birthday – was that a huge weight had finally lifted, and I felt free.

I'd successfully reshuffled my life, and I prayed that my crazy friend would give me peace to move on.

Chapter 3

Code Brown

Life is like a game of cards, it seems to me. We need to work with the hand we've been dealt, good or bad, and make the most of it.

Over the past two years, through the Covid 19 pandemic, we may all feel we have been dealt minimal cards to play the game properly. But most of us are still here, carrying on. We should make the most of life every day and play on, playing on behalf of those who are gone.

Life has changed since March 2020 for many of us, myself included – never to be the same again. But more of that later.

Back in the old school, my initiation continued. The other staff were amused by me, by my lack of knowledge of such things like football, and in particular the bigoted underworld of the Protestant/Catholic divide in the West of Scotland.

Being from the East Coast, I didn't understand some of the language and constantly waited for the end of each sentence that ended 'but…'. It seemed that it was the normal way for the West Coast folk to end a sentence.

A lot of the staff in the school were Catholic, unlike myself, and constantly joked with me that I'd only 'got in' because I had an Irish-sounding name. I had probably led quite a sheltered life in some ways and knew I suffered from naivety, believing everything I was told.
Some of the 3rd and 4th year pupils were taller than me, which didn't do anything for my confidence. During a particularly rowdy lunchtime, I shouted at a 4th year boy, 'What's your name?'
'Jonathan,' he answered quickly.
'That's enough, Jonathan!' I told him as assertively and firmly as I could, while other pupils sniggered.
Other staff seemed to be warming to me and definitely seemed to be looking out for me, always running to help when I was having trouble with challenging pupils or struggling with equipment – wheelchairs that weren't behaving, lunch trays, standing frames, feeding equipment, etc.
That day, the Headmaster approached with an aura of authority, 'What seems to be the trouble, Miss?' he asked me.
'It's Jonathan,' I confided.
'We don't have a Jonathan,' he replied.
The boys fell about laughing hysterically.
Even in the staffroom I was a constant form of amusement. A teacher disclosed to me one day, 'Did you know the word 'gullible' isn't even in the dictionary?' There was much hilarity when I repeated this fact in the staffroom, of course. So, I was going to have to 'pull my socks up' and find some credibility from somewhere.
At home I had a long look in the mirror and started to see what others were seeing. A small 'mousey' person stared back at me, looking very smart and well dressed with matching pastel coloured blouse and cardigan, long flowing skirt and chunky wedge shoes. A pink flowery scarf sat around her hair, tied in a perfect bow.

A teacher once commented about my shoes, 'You need to watch out for the Minnie Mouse effect.'
That was me: I was Minnie Mouse.
This look seemed to go down well with the younger pupils, and they definitely seemed to be 'warming' to me, but I was beginning to understand why I was a constant source of amusement to older pupils.
Respect is not a gift; it has to be earned.

One woman seemed to have taken a total dislike to me. Another member of the School Support team, she would do her best to ignore me when I spoke, talk over me, or stand in front of me if we were gathered in a group.
It was a form of bullying, and as it got worse I realised that I was going to have to confront her. It was something I dreaded and caused me a lot of anxiety.
But the atmosphere between us was bad, and that was something I was going to have to address.
Eventually, I decided to confront her.
I confided in a colleague who had started the same day as myself. We'd been terrified at first in this scary new environment and had become quite close, physically hanging onto each other in the first few weeks.
We were very different, but in a strange way we seemed to complement each other. However, she'd managed to fit in better than I had.
She had a forthright, 'don't mess with me' kind of attitude that I admired, while I was more the diplomat, advising her to hold back at times and think before she spoke.

I'd joked in the staff room one day about my shocking experiences working during the 2001 Census, and mentioned some of the homes and people I'd visited in an area in the next town.

'Tick the relevant box on the forms if you are unable to deliver the Census form,' we had been told at the training day. 'We need to know why the form was not delivered.'
The only problem with that was there was no box on the form to tick for:

1. Children home alone without any adults present;
2. Lady was too inebriated to accept the form;
3. Large German Shepherd dog guarding the property;

And my personal favourite...

4. Gentleman was locked inside the property by his wife as she was out at the Bingo and she was worried he would get out and buy alcohol. (He had explained this to me through the letterbox.)

Unfortunately, these comments didn't go down too well with my new friend at school, as it was the area of the town she'd been brought up in. However, she seemed to forgive me, and she listened intently when I told her about my problem with our colleague.
'I've noticed that,' she agreed. 'You do need to do something, and she'll get a shock 'cos she'll think you're a wee mouse.'
The following day, as if by chance, it was just the two of us sent out on a 'community visit'. That was when we were asked to take pupils outwith the school, to parks, museums, shops, or swimming. We'd normally go out in a group of three or four pupils, with staff allocated 1:1. We'd be given some money to buy juice and snacks for the pupils.
Health and safety in the early 2000's wasn't as it is today, and we had been taking pupils swimming for a number of years before we were called in and asked about the 'Moving and Handling' procedures used in getting the complex pupils to and from the bus and to/from the pool.

As School Support staff, responsible for some very challenging and vulnerable high school pupils outwith school, we found ourselves in some very testing situations. We were, of course, very professional and careful, following all procedures, but there was no need to mention such incidents as the time when we were all asked to exit the pool when pool attendants called to each other on their walkie-talkies, 'Code brown, code brown, everybody out!'

There was another incident during our trip to the swimming baths when a pupil barged into the changing cubicle of another pupil who was completely undressed. Staff dealt with the situation well, explaining to both pupils why that wasn't acceptable and why it shouldn't happen again. However, unknown to everyone, the pupil who had barged in had a very strong sense of guilt as he boarded the bus ready to return to school that day. He obviously felt it only fair and just that he should show the other pupil his private parts in return. We didn't see that coming...

On another school outing, we visited a large country park with playparks, museums, a café, and an area with small animals and fish. That was the day that we realised one of the pupils in the group suffered with ornithophobia.

As we entered the café, a large, ornate bird cage sat on a table in the café, with a brightly coloured parrot inside.

'Pretty boy, pretty boy,' the bird said as we entered the café.

Immediately, Stephen freaked, ran right out the café, across the car park, and up the hill!

Staff were allocated 1:1 so this was a dangerous situation. If two staff were to chase him, this would leave another member of staff responsible for two pupils. But this was an emergency situation, so the staff gave chase.

We managed to catch Stephen and bring him back to the café. By that time, a member of the café staff had put a cover over the cage, so all was quiet and we managed to persuade Stephen back inside.

Still, he was nervous and afraid. We talked to him and tried to persuade him everything was safe, all was ok, the parrot was in the cage, and it couldn't get out. But he continued to be very anxious and refused any juice or snacks.

I tried out a strategy that I'd seen the Headmaster use.

'Stephen, give me your worries,' I said very firmly. 'Give me them, put them right here in my hands, and I'll take them from you and look after them.'

I held both my hands out and stared confidently and intently at him.

'It's ok, I'll take your worries and I'll have them, and you will feel better.'

I'd seen the Headmaster use this in school and been in awe at how he managed to make it work with the pupils.

Slowly Stephen reached forward and placed his imaginary bundle of worries in my hands. Tears welled up and stung my eyes. What a success! I'd learned a great strategy, and it worked. I felt emotional and proud.

Stephen, though, still watched the bird cage.

I had an idea that I'd show him that the bird **was indeed** inside the cage. I would show him from afar, and he'd see that the bird was safely locked inside the cage and couldn't get out.

I prepared him step by step. 'I'm going to take the cover off now, and you'll see that the bird is safely locked inside the cage, Stephen. Look and see.'

The café staff had closed up and were clearing up behind the scenes.

I took the cover off, and to my shock and horror there was no bird in the cage. It was completely empty!!
'Oh sorry,' the café lady said, 'I took him away earlier when I saw your boy was afraid.'
Stephen ran to the bus screaming, and we followed.

Chapter 4

Never Work with Children or Animals

So, there was nothing else for it… I'd confront the woman who I felt was bullying me. I'd talk to her; I'd sort this out; it would be simple.

She scared me a bit, though. She was definitely harder than me (although that wasn't difficult), and she had scarlet coloured hair and a husky voice.

That day we walked together in silence, both pushing our pupils in wheelchairs. There were no 'niceties' and no conversation. Not a word was spoken.

We reached the shopping centre, and I said, 'Look, what is your problem with me? You obviously have a problem.'

She turned suddenly, her eyes red and fiery, and snapped, 'WHAT?'

This was not the look or the reaction I had expected, but I carried on.

'Look, I know you have a problem with me,' I said sheepishly. 'Just tell me if I've done something. I like to work well with people. I like to get along with people, and I don't like an atmosphere.'

She flicked her scarlet hair back angrily with a deeply tanned hand. 'I don't know what you're talking about!' she replied. But she was rattled, and I could tell she was raging at me.

She turned the wheelchair around abruptly and stormed off, leaving me behind. This was totally against health and safety policy, as we were supposed to stay together.

I felt sick in the pit of my stomach as I walked slowly back to the school. How would I explain this, if I was asked why we didn't stay together? Why didn't we return together?

This was all so new to me. And once again I felt totally out of my depth.

Things had been so much easier when I was at home childminding. There I was in control. I was providing a service from my home. It allowed me to look after my own children and be there for them if they were sick, while also caring for other folk's children to allow them to go to work.

But my girls were both at high school now, and the youngest of the children I had looked after (the twins) had started school. So, I'd decided it was time for me to get a job outside the home.

In fairness, though, it hadn't always been easy in the beginning, I suppose. We had no family when we moved here, and no-one to look after our girls if we had both gone out to work. So I'd chosen to stay home.

However, other parents noticed this, and I was regularly asked if I could look after someone's kids.

A friend who had decided to go back to work as a teacher one day a week asked if I would take her son for that one day, and she would pay me. Only one day, one child; I could do that. How difficult could it be?

It was a Wednesday. But it got that I dreaded a Wednesday, because the boy was so badly behaved and unruly, and he was hitting my daughter. I found it extremely stressful, but his mother was my friend. What a difficult situation.

I didn't want to lose my first friend.

The Wednesdays got worse. He was constantly taking toys from my daughter and hitting her if she wouldn't give them to him. I was becoming more and more stressed and dreading the Wednesdays. I was trying to be diplomatic, negotiating with him, peacekeeping, but Wednesdays were becoming like a war zone. I was reaching the end of my tether, so something was going to have to be said.

'That boy is spoiled,' my mum said one day. 'He needs a good smacking!' she informed me.

'Mum, we're not allowed to smack kids anymore,' I told her.

'Rubbish!' she announced. 'Never did you any harm.'

I found myself dreading the Wednesdays so much that it spoiled my whole week.

One bright, sunny June afternoon, the kids were out in the back garden, and I'd stepped into the kitchen to put the kettle on.

Urgent, terrified screams came immediately from the back garden, and I ran out to find my daughter with a red mark across her face and crying hysterically.

'What happened?' I asked her. 'Tell me what happened.'

Through sobs, she told me that the boy had hit her on the face to get her toy.

Enough was enough...

'GO AND HIT HIM BACK!' I found myself shouting. 'GO AND HIT HIM RIGHT NOW!'

It may not have been the right advice to give to my daughter in hindsight, but it came from frustration and anger, and a sense of letting my own child down by bringing this badly behaved boy into our home week after week and subjecting her to this abuse. It was her own home, a place where she should have been safe.

She did hit him back, as he cowered against the fence in horror.

And we didn't have to worry about Wednesdays again after that. He told his mum what happened that afternoon, and she didn't bring him again.

I didn't see my friend much after that, but I did have a dream about her a while later. I dreamed she had someone locked in her basement and that there was a 'For Sale' sign on the house. The dream was so strong and vivid that I decided to pay her a visit to tell her about it.

We sat outside in the sunshine, drinking cool lemonade, and I told her about my dream and how vivid it had been.

'We have no plans to move,' she laughed. 'But you must have heard what happened with the electrician?'

'No,' I said curiously.

'Oh dear. It was an accident. The kids were running in and out of the basement when the electrician was working, so I told him I'd just turn the key in the lock so he would have peace to work, and he should just knock when he was finished... I went out and forgot all about him.'

Her husband had heard the tired knocking at midnight!

I suppose this situation wouldn't happen nowadays, but in the 90s mobile phones weren't so common or as reliable. The poor guy may well have had a chunky mobile phone sitting on the front seat of his little van.

A while after that I heard from another woman at our Mother & Toddler group that a rich American man had knocked on my friend's door and made them an offer for their house that they couldn't refuse. They'd moved out within a week.

We never saw them again.

It wasn't easy making new friends, and I remember the look on a neighbour's face one day as I sat in the back garden with my daughter when she was only a few months old.

The lady was elderly, and she had a little white Scotty dog that she walked slowly up the lane at the back of the house.

'Have you not got any friends, dear?' she asked me with a very perplexed look on her face.

I recalled that look on her face for a long time, and it haunted me.

But it took time to make friends.

By the time my daughter was about six months old, I began to get to know other young mums through Mother & Toddler groups. There was also a very useful group called 'The National Childbirth Trust' that had (and still does, as far as I know) local groups in every city and town to put parents in touch with each other.

A friend from Fife gave me a contact number when we knew we were moving to Glasgow.

There was a huge difference in childcare between the 80s and 90s. In the 80s the Mother & Toddler groups and playgroups were stretched to capacity with waiting lists, and almost 100% of the childcare was done by parents, with an occasional nanny or childminder.

Within a few years into the 90s, everything was changing, and more mothers were returning to work to pay for the astronomical mortgage increases. Ours sat at 15.5% interest, I remember. At one point I thought we'd lose our house.

The switch in childcare in the 90s was obvious, as nearly everyone bringing the children to the Mother & Toddler groups were either childminders, nannies, or Grannies.

I found myself very much in the minority, so I decided to have a proper 'go' at childminding. I'd do it properly this time, though, and get myself registered as a childminder and take training courses. It would be another way of getting to know people and to learn skills such as First Aid training.

I was also the emergency contact for a number of the kids at the local primary school by then, as I was at home, and more and more women were heading back to work.

I remember getting a phone call from the school office lady one day, asking if I could come to the school. She was hesitant and vague, and I asked what had happened. Had my friend's daughter had some kind of accident?

'No, not exactly,' I was told. 'If you could just come and collect her hamster.' It appears the hamster had 'climbed into her schoolbag' that day unnoticed!

A local woman I knew came to my door one day and asked if I'd look after her daughter. The little girl was a year older than our younger daughter, so she was three years old, and I thought this could be a good friendship between the girls.

On the first day, she was dropped off at the house and my task was to take her to the local playgroup and then pick her up again after.

Easy, or so I thought.

However, this child had been lifted and laid by car everywhere she went and hadn't had to walk anywhere.

'What colour is your car?' she asked me innocently, as we all got ready to go, putting warm coats on, my daughter in her sturdy Silver Cross buggy.

'Oh, I don't have a car,' I informed her. 'We're walking today.'

I could tell immediately that this was not going down well.

'I don't walk,' she told me.

She was right. She didn't walk. And it took us twice as long as normal to get along a normal ten-minute walk that day. Halfway there, she sat down on the pavement and refused to move. So I was eventually forced to let the little princess into the buggy while my two-year-old daughter walked the rest of the way.

She came for a number of years, and she did get better at walking.

One day the school called me to come and collect her, as she was unwell, and they were unable to get in touch with her parents.

I brought her home and tucked her up in my daughter's bed, warm and cosy, while I tried to get in touch with her mum or dad on their mobile phones. All day I tried unsuccessfully.

Then, around 4 o'clock (an hour earlier than normal) I saw her mum parking her car outside.

Great, I thought, at last the wee one would get home to her own bed.

I stood at the upstairs window watching her mum get out of the car and walk to our gate. She had a quick look at her watch, hesitated, and then walked back to the car, got in, and drove off. Clearly, she wasn't going to lose an hour of childminding she'd paid for!

Over the years, I had an interesting group of children, including a prankster who took it upon himself to hide when his mum came to collect him. And that was embarrassing.

'Of course I haven't lost your son. Just take a seat and I'll go find him... I mean, call him.'

Then there were the dreams. My husband said he didn't want to hear about my dreams after a while.

I remember drifting off to sleep one night, just relaxing into that comfortable loose state, when BAM! I sat bolt upright in bed, shocked and breathing heavily, then I screamed out.

'What's wrong?' my husband asked. 'What is it?'

I'd had a vision. A vision of my little prankster, and his face was covered in blood – thick, red, sticky blood. My heart was racing. Why would I dream such a thing? What was wrong with me!?

'This is bad,' I told my husband. 'This is a bad omen"

'Not at all, it's nothing,' he reassured me. 'You were dreaming.'

Later that same week, the prankster was in a fight in school with another boy. The boy slammed him into a wall and split his head open. There was thick, red, sticky blood all over his face and across the back of his head, His smart school jumper was red and sticky, and all the smaller children I was caring for stared at it with their mouths open.

'Do not tell me anything more about your dreams,' my husband announced that evening. 'No more.'

It wasn't all plain sailing, now I look back. On one occasion I offered to look after my friend's dog. We didn't have a dog ourselves, but growing up we'd had a couple in the family.

It was the day after my friend's wedding, and a wonderful wedding it was. We didn't know her new husband well or the dog, but how difficult could it be?

He was a black and white collie dog, and very clever, but we had no idea what age he was.

Our girls weren't used to having a dog around, so it was a real novelty for them. I watched from my mum's garden as our oldest daughter took the collie onto the grassy area across the road and picked up a big stick for him to fetch.

She raised her arm to throw the stick as far as she could... but she was still holding him on the lead.

'LET HIM OFF THE LEAD!' I shouted.

Too late! The dog took off at top speed, and she was left face down in the mud.

Later, we drove to the golf club to pick up my hubby.

'That's not my car,' he said out loud to no-one in particular. 'It can't be, 'cos we don't have a dog.'

'It's only for a few days,' I promised. 'There was no-one else to take him.'

Hubby was not happy, but he did grow to like the dog over the following days, and there was no doubt that the dog loved him. The dog would jump the fence each day to meet him as he came home from work.

He was a working dog and constantly circled the children, rounding them up, keeping them safe. He even woke me each morning like a proper gentleman – nudging my arm gently to wake me.

However, it was the last day that he was with us that things went wrong.

It was a beautiful, hot, sunny day and all the children were in the garden playing – my own children and the ones I was childminding.

Hubby drove up the lane at the back of the house, and the dog tried to jump the fence as he had done every day. But this time something went wrong.

He'd somehow not cleared the fence and managed to impale himself on one of the spikes. It was horrific. Those screams the dog made will go to the grave with me – and with the children, probably.

Our lovely friend appeared at the door unexpectedly and probably wished she hadn't. With her help, we managed to bundle him into a blanket, and slowly and gently get him into her campervan to take him to the vet.

Poor old boy. He survived the incident, but our friends still recall how the East Coast family would comment, 'Aye, the poor dug has never been the same since it went to Glesga and got stabbed.'

So here I was, walking back to school, with a weight around my shoulders. Had I breached policy? Was I about to be disciplined? Sacked? Battered by my scarlet-haired colleague at the gates at 3 o'clock? My legs shook, and I felt physically sick.

It was lunchtime, and it was time for a changeover of staff. But something had clearly been said, as there was an atmosphere that could be cut with a butter knife, and looks exchanged between staff members.

Scarlet was there, saying nothing.

It was all too much. A member of staff laid a hand on my shoulder and told me to go for my lunch.

I jumped up off the seat like it was on fire, stumbling, and knocked over a lunch tray, splattering a steak pie lunch onto the floor and up the wall. A pupil took the opportunity to grab a carton of milk and squeezed it hard, bursting it open and drenching a colleague in icy cold milk. The pupil laughed and laughed; it was her party trick.

In my rush to leave the dinner hall, I tripped over a wheelchair foot plate, catching another pupil's trainer, and it flew off across the hall.

It was all too much... I had to get out of the building, had to get air.

I grabbed my coat from the staffroom, tears blinding me as I dashed up the corridor. From behind me, a number of staff were following.

The Deputy came out of her office and took my arm. 'What's wrong, what's happened?' she asked kindly.

But I had to get out.

Staff members followed me outside into the street, but I kept walking. A female member of staff who had never spoken to me before, took my arm and walked with me, as tears streamed down my face.

'Don't go,' she said softly. 'You can't go, we need you.'

'But I'm rubbish at this job, you won't miss me,' I sobbed.

'The kids love you,' she said quietly, and all at once I stopped and looked at her. 'And we love you. You're a funny wee thing with your funny wee ways, but please don't go. You're just like wee Bella from the Tweenies. I think I'll call you Bella.'

We stood hugging then, tears blinding us both. She had the strongest, warmest, most sincere hug I'd ever felt, and I believed her.

Chapter 5

Thank you for the music

Music played a big part of my teenage years. My cousin and I waited patiently for 6 o'clock every Sunday night to hear the Top 20 on Radio One. We would try to tape it on the old cassette player every Sunday, but it was a tricky business as we would have to set up the radio AND a cassette player at the same time to record. Then we would need to find somewhere quiet where the grown-ups weren't talking, so that we could tape through the little red microphone. It was all very technical.

We had to make sure that there was an empty cassette tape available to use for taping over. And sometimes, after a while, we'd look and see that the whole tape had unravelled inside the cassette player and we had lost everything. That meant we'd need to wait a whole week and try again the following Sunday.

We loved the sounds of the 70s: Elvis, of course – 'Love Me Tender', 'Blue Suede Shoes'; Mud; Showaddywaddy, 'Three Steps to Heaven'; The Osmonds, (especially Donny with his 'Puppy Love' that still brings butterflies to my stomach today); David Cassidy; Candi Statton with 'Young Hearts Run Free'; John Lennon's 'Imagine', and of course, Elton, David Bowie, Marc Bolan. Not forgetting Olivia Newton-John and John Travolta in *Grease* – 'You're the One That I Want' – that final scene in the movie a total classic.

I absolutely loved 'Pig Bag' for some unknown reason, but the heavy, raspy sound of the saxophone and the hard beat of the drums just made me want to get up and dance, even if I was the only one on the dance floor. It was overpowering and hypnotising, and I could feel the music through me.

And who could forget the great Scottish band, the Bay City Rollers? I loved the Rollers, and I confess to being one of the tartan-clad, crazy fans to this day.

My best friend Susan and I talked about it recently, and we reminisced about the songs and the band and the incredible following they had in the 70s.

We shared our sadness of the outcome of how the boys seemed to have been ripped off by their manager in the 70s and left penniless. Yet their songs still fill dance floors to this day.

'They're still touring, you know,' she informed me. 'The Rollers.'

'No! Really?' I couldn't believe it after all these years. Why didn't I know this?

A few days later, I got an ominous text message from Susan. *What are you doing on the 13th of November?*

Nothing, I replied.

Great, well we're going to see the Rollers.

When we were dropped off outside the great Glasgow Barrowlands in heavy rain that night, we didn't expect the crowds, stretching right along the road and round the block for four streets. It was a mass of tartan-clad, crazy Roller's fans, excited to be there, reliving their youth. There were accents from all over, from Caithness to Dublin, Inverness to Newcastle.

What an amazing sight and an amazing night. Women of all ages, four generations of families – grannies, mums, daughters, and granddaughters – singing along to 'Shang-a-Lang' and 'Summer Love Sensation', waving their tartan scarves and trying to touch one of the band – the favourite was the lead singer, Les McKeown. There were even 50-year-old women passing out, lying on the alcohol-drenched floor.

All around us was a sea of tartan and happy faces, eyes shining bright, scarves above our heads, swaying to the music. We were 14 again and singing along to 'Bye Bye Baby' without a care in the world. Dancing along to 'The Bump' with random fans.

What a fantastic night!

It was all a bit different from the first time I visited the great Glasgow Barrowlands. I'm looking at the old ticket stub now: 19th November, 1998. Twenty years earlier.

It was advertised in a Sunday newspaper, and I was so happy with myself finding it. It was supposed to be a Christmas present, but I was very bad at keeping secrets. How long could I keep it from my husband?

Weeks went by, and I was very pleased with myself that I hadn't let anything slip.

'Some of the lads are going to this concert on the 19th,' he confided one night.

'You don't want to go see some ancient band, do you?' I fobbed him off.

'Suppose not,' he said, looking disappointed.

He'd been to lots of concerts over the years and bought the t-shirts of course. Most were neatly folded and living in the bottom drawer of the old chest of drawers. Led Zeppelin, Sammy Hagar, Genesis, The Jam. They no longer fitted, but I daren't throw them out.

I'll never forget my own first ever concert, 'Kid Creole & the Coconuts,' in The Edinburgh Playhouse, October 17th, 1982. I loved Kid Creole, loved the Latin-American style of music. He'd bought me the tickets and we were supposed to go together, but it didn't happen that way as he was strung up like a piece of meat in the hospital on the day of the concert, so I went with his sister.

As the weeks came closer, I decided I couldn't keep the secret any longer and threw the tickets across the dinner table at him one night.

A hard frost was settling on the parked cars that night as we stood queuing outside the Barrowlands. Ticket touts were running up and down the line, buying and selling unwanted tickets.

I'd wrapped up warm with a heavy coat on, fleecy gloves, and scarf. Hubby was frisked as we reached the door, and I was asked to empty out my old denim handbag. Some used paper hankies, a few mouldy conkers, a Duplo Grandma, and a couple of babies' dummies came flying out, and I got the feeling that wasn't what the bouncer had been expecting. I was starting to feel that this was going to be very different from other concerts I'd been to.

We followed the crowd up the hard black stairs, past a colourless couch on the landing. The couch held onto secrets of the past, young soldiers smooching with their sweethearts and gangsters of the 60s. I could see the ghosts of the past, the Glasgow hard men with their flick-knives out, the women screaming and then blood spreading out like fine red wine across the cold black floor.

We made our way up another flight and into an empty hall.

'Where are all the seats?' I asked innocently.

'Are we not getting a seat?'

No answer.

We watched folk come in, as the hall slowly filled up. They were mostly folk in their 40s, some younger, some older. A guy in an expensive looking suit: had he just come from work? An older couple kissed intimately without shame, as if they were the only people in the room. Married perhaps, but not to each other?

'Hope he doesn't need a pee in a hurry!' hubby said, laughing.

I looked over to see a very skinny lad wearing huge Doc Martin boots, laced up to his knees, and tartan trousers covered in zips.

'He'll not know which one it's in!' he laughed at his own joke.

It was getting uncomfortable in the hall and very warm, so I handed hubby my heavy coat, scarf, and gloves.

Suddenly, the lights went out, and there were shadows on the stage. We waited. People were pushing and shoving to get to the front.

Then the lights went up and there was music.

This guy came from nowhere and stood right next to me. I tried to hide my horror at the terrible burns on his face, but I felt that my own face would betray me. Everything around me faded away, and I wondered what kind of accident could cause these burns. A firework gone wrong, or a cigarette lighter?

He pulled a cigarette from his pocket and placed it in his lipless mouth, then he squeezed past me and pushed his way to the front. I could see his face lit up from the stage lights, and he was completely absorbed by the music.

On stage were The Supernaturals – they were the support band, and they were going down well with the crowd. The women screamed as the platinum blond keyboard player ran across the stage, jumped over his keyboard, and continued to play.

When the band went off, the lights went up, I searched for the guy with the face in the crowd. But he was gone. We'd been there for two hours, standing, holding jackets. More people were piling into the hall, and it was very uncomfortable now.

'I could do with a seat,' I said. 'How much longer 'til the band comes on?'

After another long wait, the lights went out again – and they seemed to be off for a long time. There were shadows on the stage moving about, and eventually the lights went up and the great Deborah Harry ran onto the stage, looking as youthful and radiant as ever. Finally, after two hours' waiting, they were here in the flesh – the phenomenal, ageless Blondie. The audience went completely wild, folk above us surfing the crowd, a woman beside me hyperventilating. Plastic cups of beer were thrown into the air. Huge 40-year-old guys were pogoing about, beer in hand.

The band played 'The Tide is High' and the crowd mimicked the tide, singing loudly, moving back and forward like the ocean.

I found myself heading out in a beer-washed sea of unknown faces between the boy with the burns and the guy with the tartan trousers, drowning in the tide. I was going under and couldn't make my way back to safety.

From nowhere, a strong hand grabbed me and pulled me close. Hubby stood with elbows out, protecting me like a human lifebelt in the sea of faces. He stood firm, holding onto me and the winter coats, gloves, and scarves. And for another two hours we stood there, trying to enjoy the music, attempting to hold fast.

It's been a long time since that concert now. I think about all the characters I saw that night, and I realise that it wasn't them who were out of place – it was me. I was quite literally out of my depth in a world where I didn't belong.

I loved the discos when I was young. There was nothing better than being absorbed in the loud music with friends. A boy could come up behind you and tap your shoulder, asking if he could dance with you. It was up to you whether you agreed or not, depending on whether you liked the look of him.

Even then, in the 70s, it wasn't advisable to leave a drink lying and go back to it for fear it might be 'spiked'. We would take our handbags with us and put them on the floor in front of us, keeping an eye on them.

I don't know what it was about the disco nights that was so exciting and intriguing. The dark corners where you could hide away checking out the talent, watch all the good dancers, listening to the overly loud music.

But it was a different world – one I definitely did want to be included in.

Starting with the Saturday afternoon discos, it became a big part of my life.

What would you wear? There would be much deliberation and chatting with friends. The jeans were extreme – the baggier the better; and the shoes were high – the higher the better. Large, clumpy wedge shoes we called 'bumper cars' for obvious reasons, and then the jewellery – huge hoop earrings, the bigger the better. All very dangerous of course, and ankles suffered many twists over the years through falls. Tartan strips, of course, sewn onto jackets and trousers, bearing testament to the great Bay City Rollers.

My hair began to darken in the teenage years, so going on the advice from the older girls in the school toilets, I bought a bottle of peroxide from the local chemist. I was of course in deep trouble when Mum discovered what I'd done, as I'd not only bleached my hair white but all the bathroom towels and carpet as well.

I wanted the David Bowie look, with short, spiky hair, but Dad said 'no'. He hardly ever laid down the law – only saying no to the haircut, and to my sister and I getting a bike. We were definitely not allowed a bike, as he said that he saw too many kids getting knocked down in road accidents.

He was a driving Instructor and he had his own company. He was always cool and calm, never seemed to get flustered, and managed to get many thousands of people through a driving test over the years. He taught my mum and my sister, and I looked forward to the day when he would teach me. Dad always spoke quietly and gently, and he was funny. He made us laugh. He taught me how to burp at random – a skill I still possess – much to the disgust of my mum at the time.

Saturday nights at the great Kinema Ballroom was split in two – one half of the dancefloor for over 18s (the bar end) and the other half for under 18s. We loved it. Busloads of young people came from Glasgow, Stirling, and all the villages nearby. I'd go some Saturdays with my cousin and some Saturdays with a friend.

Upstairs we could get a cardboard dish of curry, or chips, or corned beef stovies (a great Scottish delicacy of mashed potatoes, corned beef, and onion).

Sometimes the music would stop, and the bouncers would all go running, then we'd see fists flying and blood splattered across the floor. The dancing would stop until the floor was cleaned up and the fighters ejected.

Sometimes my friends would run to me telling me it was my crazy friend. And he once told me in confidence that he loved the sight of blood.

Dad would be waiting for us every week after the disco. He'd park just out of sight in a side street, waiting discretely to take us home.

One night stands out in my memory – 25th April, 1976. The weather had been awful, the wind howled, and the rain lashed heavily on our faces as we walked the short distance to find Dad. Rubbish blew across the road, chip wrappers, empty cans, and cigarette packets. Scruffy mongrels were finishing what folk had left in the gutters.

Our ears buzzed from the loud disco music for hours after we left.

April had been wild; it seemed to be one storm after another, no sign of spring coming. It had been a long winter. Floods had been bad, and there had been many road accidents and fatalities.

Our neighbours had reported seeing some kind of flaming rock coming out of the sky and crashing into a chimney, setting it on fire, like a bolt out of the blue!

We were 15. Another year maybe, we reckoned, and we would be able to come home on our own, get a taxi like grown-ups.

That night, I sat in the front seat of Dad's car and Jill sat in the back. She was repeating a school year so was a year older than me, but it didn't seem to matter. We'd become good friends. I loved how tall and graceful she was and her beautiful, speckled green eyes. We had a lot of fun together.

We giggled as Dad pretended to miss the gearstick and grabbed my knees, tickling me. He sang 'Green Green Grass of Home' at the top of his voice – his favourite song by Tom Jones – and explained to us why he loved it so much and what it was about.

We dropped Jill home, and she ran quickly to get out of the rain, waving excitedly from her doorway. Before we drove off, Dad took my hand, placed it on the gearstick, then put his strong, tanned hand on top, guiding me through the gears.

'Not long now,' he told me.

When we got home, I crept quietly into bed, so that I didn't wake Gran. Her huge bosom rose and fell in the other single bed, and her snoring sounded like a never-ending motorbike.

'It's only for a short time,' I overheard Mum telling Dad, 'til she's on her feet again. We won't always have her staying here.'

I don't know what time it was – maybe 1 o'clock, 2 o'clock. I don't know, but I could hear Dad roaring like an animal, an animal in pain.

I sat up in bed. Gran snored on.

I heard Mum on the phone, calling for an ambulance, and I jumped out of bed.

Like a bolt from the blue, the harsh, cruel reality dawned on me at the hospital. The nurses were great. So lovely, so caring.

'Give him a kiss,' they instructed. 'You'll regret it later if you don't.'

His face was cold, icy cold and waxy. Strange. Not like my Dad.

It all felt like a strange dream that I couldn't wake up from.

With the dawn came a silence, an unnatural calm. Nothing moved, there were no people, no cars, no wind, no rain.

It felt like the April storms had claimed another innocent victim, and above the fields rose a great vulgar sun, smiling, victorious. I felt angry. How dare it shine its happy smiling face at us on this day when we'd lost so much!

Spring had come at last, but it was different. Everything was different, and the music had died.

Chapter 6

Young Love

1982, and I felt like I'd come a long way.

I'd left school, having secured a full-time office job, and then moved to a job in the local supermarket as a receptionist. The supermarket was classed as 'large' in the 80s, and there was talk about 24-hour shopping and codes on ALL goods that would 'do away' with conventional tills as we knew them. But the shop staff laughed at such preposterous ideas.

It was one of the biggest supermarkets in Scotland, and we had food and non-food sections.

The lovely, softly spoken Deputy Manager interviewed me for the job and left me to add up an invoice. Before he left the room, he told me to take my time as he'd rather have a member of staff who was careful and a bit slower but got things right. I was slow **and** got the numbers wrong, but somehow I got the job.

The supermarket was only one short bus ride for me, in the town, so it was much more convenient than my first job. And I loved it. I was fast on the bulky, old-fashioned switchboard, had a good memory for numbers and voices, and could remember many of the numbers used daily without looking them up, which made me really quick.

I worked there for 11 years and saw many staff come and go, and many managers come and go. During that time, I got to recognise the voices of the other Store Managers and the Area Managers.

After a time, I was moved to the invoice office. But maths and calculations are not my thing, and I found this almost impossible. Top this with the fact that the company had invested in a brand-new, top-of-the-range photocopier, thinking this would cut down much of the workload. As a result, the staffing had been cut from three invoice staff to one full-time and one part-time staff.

I couldn't work the fancy new photocopier – the size of a small car – and I couldn't get my head round the invoices. There was far too much work, so not to admit defeat I took invoices home with me every night, every weekend. But still I was weeks behind in the work.

I was becoming more and more stressed and couldn't sleep. And it was during this time that I moved to the little flat with my crazy friend.

It was all extremely bad timing.

After things came to a head with the ex and I moved back in with my mum, it became very obvious he was not going to let me live in peace. The house phone rang constantly and he stood outside the house, just watching and waiting, leaving me feeling extremely vulnerable.

My mum and her friend were due to go on holiday, and I didn't feel it was safe for me to stay. I was constantly afraid, constantly on edge.

I decided to go and stay with my sister for a week, so I requested a week off work. Looking back, I was probably having a bit of a breakdown.

While I was off work, it became clear to the boss that the job was not actually viable with the reduced staff, and new staff were brought in. I worked on in Invoicing alongside the new staff, and after a while I was promoted to Assistant Personnel Officer.

My duties included preparing the overtime payments and reporting absences, etc, to Head Office. I also had to make up the 250 brown envelope wage packets every week, and provide a bit of pastoral care, training, and interviewing part time staff.

I love people (mostly), so I loved all the interaction with the staff.

I remember commenting at the start of one interview about the lovely tan the young girl had, only to be told that her dad was Spanish!

My personal life was growing and glowing, as I discovered my crazy friend was wrong – and people actually did like me. Boys definitely did, and every week at the end of the night I had at least one offer of a walk home.

I'd met a lovely group of friends through one of these boys, and two of the girls were looking for a flatmate to help them pay the rent on their extremely classy, rented flat in a nice area of town. It was perfect. Two lovely girls who I became great friends with, and it also got me away from the crazy one.

I did see him a few times at the Kinema Ballroom, but I told my flatmates about him and they were very protective of me. He'd come and stand really close, too close to where we were sitting, and I suffered with the whole 'fight or flight' dilemma. Would I stand my ground, or would I just leave? He looked so smug, so happy to know he was making me feel awkward, and I hoped that he couldn't see my legs shaking beneath the table.

At that time I was seeing a boy who lived in the next street. He had beautiful blond, curly hair and a motorbike. I wasn't crazy about him, but I had to admit having a boyfriend with a motorbike was exciting. It took me a few dates to learn how to dress for a motorbike, though – the very tight, maroon velvet pencil skirt definitely wasn't suitable!

Previously I'd dated a boy with a little sports car. I really did like him and was devastated when he 'chucked' me. It seems he was three-timing me, all with girls the same name as mine. I had to hand it to him - that was clever.

Some boys who shared the flat in the next street were having a party. We knew them a bit, and one of them was a good friend of sports car boy. One night, sports car boy came to visit me to apologise for the three-timing situation and introduced his very tall friend to me – the friend from the flat in the next street. I wasn't interested in apologies or his friend, and they were asked to leave.

We decided we would go to the party, though. No point in missing a good party!

What I didn't know was that tall guy had found out that curly motorbike boy was going on holiday when the party was on. It seems, tall guy made an 'off the cuff' comment to Curly.

'That's very brave of you,' he laughed, 'leaving that wee bird of yours. I might just take her off your hands.'

Curly didn't respond, I heard.

That night, my flatmate looked slim and elegant as we got ready for the party. She wore a strapless, glittery top and tight-fitting, skinny jeans. Her hair was dark and glossy.

'What about the tall guy?' I asked her quietly as we added the finishing touches to our make-up. 'He looks like your type.'

'Hmm...' She waved her hand dismissively. 'He's alright, I suppose.'

I'd been 'comfort eating' and knew I had put on a fair bit of weight. Eating that junk food to make myself feel better meant the little pink cotton dress I'd bought was very tight around my hips. A young workman whistled at me one day in the town, a 'wolf whistle'. But I clearly heard his pal say, 'Ewwww, what, that fat bird?' That didn't do anything for my confidence, of course.

I had also been having problems with skin infections and been given numerous antibiotics to try and clear that up. So, I wasn't feeling at my best for sure, but hopefully after a couple of drinks I'd feel better.

We could hear the music from the party as we turned into the street that night, and folk were spilling out of the house and into the garden. As we pushed our way past the crowds milling about on the outside staircase, I caught sight of sports car boy with his new girlfriend. The butterflies in my stomach took hold, and I needed a drink to settle them.

Two tall glasses of cider and Babycham later, I was feeling more confident and decided to 'fix up' my flatmate with the tall guy. He was deep in conversation with an older man – I've no idea what they were talking about – but I took the decision to sit myself down on his lap.

He turned to look at me, and all at once he grinned and I could see his warm, brown speckled eyes smiling at me. His strong arm wrapped around my waist as he continued to chat with the older guy.

It felt strong and safe and right. Completely right.

That was not what I'd expected – not at all. And all of a sudden I decided I wouldn't be suggesting he date my flatmate. I'd keep him to myself.

As I sat there with him, sports car guy came past and stopped.

'He's the one for you,' he confided, nodding at me drunkenly. 'I know he is. He's better for you than me. He'll make you happy.'

The tall guy walked me home that night, and we stood talking for hours – him on the bottom step and me two steps up so we were 'eye to eye'.

'Bye then,' he said eventually. 'See ya.'

Was that it? I was confused. What just happened? Was it over as quickly as it had started?

Chapter 7

Like a Prayer

July 1982:

The night after the party, I got ready for bed as usual. I took the old Kirby grips out of the little china trinket box and pinned back my fringe so that the antibiotic cream wouldn't go all over my hair. The swelling was going down, and the skin was starting to look better.

I stared in the mirror at the ghostly figure in the long, white nighty. No wonder the tall guy hadn't been in touch. I looked a mess. Tears mixed with antibiotic cream and dripped onto my nightie, and I settled into bed with a magazine and a chocolate bar to console myself.

Just as I was about to switch the light off, the doorbell rang. The doorbell never rang this late on a Sunday night, so my flatmates and I were sent into a frenzy, running about trying to see from the bedroom window who was at the door.

We struggled to find the big key for the heavy front door, and as I pulled it open, I don't know who got more of a fright, him or me! It was after 11pm, but he didn't seem to think anything of the time, and he came inside, and we chatted for hours over several cups of tea.

'Bye then, see ya,' he said after a while. And from the big bay window I watched him running the full length of the street so fast, as if the devil was chasing him.

We saw each other every day after that, often at 11pm after he'd been to five-a-side football and he'd hobble in with numerous injuries.

October 1982:
I was honoured when he mentioned going to meet his parents, but I just hadn't expected the journey to be so far. I didn't know you could drive for six hours and still be in Scotland. They were kind and polite, but I didn't feel relaxed at all.
We were only there for a couple of days, and I was given his sister's bedroom with a 'cabin type' bed. It was strange sleeping so near the ceiling.
There was multi-coloured wallpaper on all the walls and ceiling, but I couldn't quite make out the pattern. I was beginning to worry about my eyesight, and thought I'd need to get myself an appointment to get an eye test when we got back home.
I lay awake staring at that ceiling, wondering about my tall guy. Was he 'the one' for me? My special someone who I'd spend the rest of my life with? I liked him. I liked him a lot, but did I love him?
How would I know? How does anyone know? I hadn't prayed for such a long time, but maybe my God would have the answer.
'Lord God,' I prayed, 'is this tall guy the right one for me? Can you send me a sign?'
Nothing. I waited, nothing. No sign came.
My life had no pattern, no definition. Just like the wallpaper, it wasn't at all clear.

A blanket of thick black cloud loomed over us as we said our goodbyes the next day and headed south. A patchwork of vibrant greens and yellows, separated by Caithness flagstone dykes, stood out in front of us, flat and even, into the distance. A field of sheep appeared now and again, a single solitary tree, bent over by the winds, a carpet of purple heather by the roadside. The scenery was wild and rough, but I could see the beauty in it.

Crystal Gayle sang out loud and clear from the old cassette player sitting on the dashboard, 'Don't You Make My Brown Eyes Blue.'

Unfamiliar road signs – Halkirk, Tongue, Latheron Wheel.

The road bent and curved round the coastline, and the sea rippled and sparkled in the sun.

'CHECK YOUR BRAKES' the sign shouted at us urgently. 'BERRIEDALE BRAES 13% GRADIENT.'

I imagined that the old Cortina wouldn't make it and we'd simply slide back down to the bottom of the steep hill.

'Welcome to Sutherland' the sign greeted us.

Black lambs were suckling from white mothers, and from the cassette player Kid Creole sang 'Annie, I'm Not Your Daddy'.

We made a stop in Brora, at the famous Italian ice cream shop.

'We should go there,' he said. 'To Italy I mean.'

'Really?' I find myself sounding like an excited five-year-old.

He looked as surprised as me, as if the words had caught him off-guard, too.

'Sure,' he confirmed, 'maybe next summer.'

'Parisienne Walkways' from the old cassette player.

My thoughts turned to summer holidays then, as I curled up on the passenger seat with my shoes off.

John Lennon told us to 'Imagine', and I dreamed of sunshine glistening on white painted walls. I could feel hot sand on my feet, see children building high sandcastles, parents fussing with suncream and sunhats...

And then BANGGGGG!!!!!!
The car was spinning round and round, like it'd never stop and my tall guy roared. A hand protected my face. Was I dreaming or was this really happening??
I opened my eyes and there was black smoke in front of us. The car was sitting on grass.
'You'll need to get out,' he stated calmly.
'Ok, you too,' I replied.
'Sure, you first,' he instructed.
I scooped up my favourite purple suede shoes, with the kitten heels and the cute bows on the front. Then I emptied the fragments of glass from inside them in a sleepy, slow-motion action.
As I walked across the grass, I was aware that my tall guy wasn't following me, and cars, buses, and lorries had all stopped on the motorway and people were running towards us.
I turned around to see the whole front of the old Cortina completely smashed in, and black smoke escaping from the hood.
A man with a cigarette walked towards the car and people shouted for him to stay back.
My tall guy couldn't get out the car; he was trapped. I started to run back, but a big, strong lorry driver stopped me and held me, saying it wasn't safe to return. And all at once I needed to be with him; must be with him. I knew I never wanted to be apart from him again... ever.
He hadn't seen the Range Rover coming. It's easily done: you pull out to have a look with a view to overtaking, but there's something right there.
The emergency services were there for two hours, cutting him out of the car, but eventually he was free and lifted into the ambulance.
'Don't forget my golf clubs!' he shouted to the firemen, and they laughed at his misplaced priorities.

We sat side by side in the ambulance, grinning at each other, tears running down both our faces.
'I think I love ya,' he said finally.
'I think I love you, too,' I said.
'I know,' he said, grinning broadly.
The paramedic inside the ambulance silently wiped a tear from her eye.

Chapter 8

People are people...

I would say that I am a 'people person'. I like spending time with people, and during my 60+ years there really haven't been many people that I can say I haven't got along with. 'It takes all kinds to make a world,' my mum would say.

People are interesting, and I think horoscopes are interesting. I bought a book about the Chinese horoscopes once and found it fascinating.

So, I was born in the year of the Ox – and the traits of those born under the sign of the Ox are that we carry heavy burdens, both physically and metaphorically, and I would totally agree with that. I am very prone to carrying loads that are too heavy for me in every way.

A Chinese friend once told me it also depends what time of the day you are born. She was born during the night when the Ox sleeps (she told me), and therefore her mother assured her she would not need to work hard. This appeared to be accurate, as her husband was wealthy and she didn't work outside the home.

I was born mid-afternoon, which is when the Ox works hardest she told me, and it does feel like I have worked hard.

1982:

In the big supermarket, a new Store Manager was appointed, and he obviously saw himself as 'a new brush sweeping clean'. Unfortunately, he created a lot of 'dust', and many staff were swept right out the door. He treated me like a 'coffee girl,' constantly calling me wherever I was and demanding coffee – strong, black coffee, ALL day, EVERY day! No matter what I was doing, I had to stop what I was doing and fetch coffee for him and any visitors he may be meeting with.

It got to me after a while, because I was actually having to come in on my days off to finish my work due to the time I was spending making coffee! But he was the big boss, so what could I do? I couldn't say 'no'. I even tried avoiding him and hiding from him, but he always seemed to find me.

I was feeling very stressed and angry, and I thought about leaving. But I loved my job and had made many good friends in the big supermarket. Why should I leave?

At the same time, I discovered one of the Supervisors in the Deli department had bought a new house. Everyone was congratulating him as he was moving in with his girlfriend.

Only... it turned out it was MY HOUSE – my little painted house with the white walls.

The carpets and furniture were stored in my boss's garage taking up space, and I knew they would fit perfectly. Perhaps I could recoup some of my savings if I sold the carpets to him.

I put this to him and asked for £100. It was a fraction of the original price, but at least I was getting something back. The guy was delighted and agreed to pay me £10 a week.

I waited, and I waited.

I got a £10, and then a second £10, and then nothing.

How could he do this to me? He'd got the carpets cheap, and they fitted perfectly. They had only been a few weeks old.

I had to ask him every week for the money, and every week I got an excuse about why he didn't have my £10.

I think I did eventually get it all, but months had passed, and I think it was actually the Personnel Officer who spoke to him after I mentioned it to her in frustration.

Another thing the new Store Manager started was to call the office staff down to 'man' the tills when the checkouts were busy or short-staffed. Again, we had to stop whatever we were doing when we were called, and make our way to the tills.

I HATED that call. For starters, the customers were irritated and annoyed by the time we got there, as they'd been waiting, and they took their bad temper out on us.

'My ice cream's melting, hen, I've been waiting here so long,' they'd moan.

'Can't you go any faster?'

Being left-handed was a significant disadvantage at the checkouts, I discovered, as they were built for a right-handed person. So it took me longer than most to sort myself out to operate the till with my right hand.

But we weren't checkout operators, so we didn't know the prices and were still depending on price stickers on everything. If the price sticker was missing, we'd then need to call for a Supervisor – which took more time.

Also, we were used to working with calculators in the offices, where a half was 'point five' on the buttons. But in those days, half pennies were still in circulation and there was a 'half pence' button on the tills.

Mostly we got that wrong and keyed in point five instead of the half pence, so it would come up on the till receipt as fifty pence instead of half a penny. And of course, that would make quite a difference to the final total.

Between running for coffee for the Store Manager, and running to help at checkouts, my work was suffering and I was becoming more stressed.

In the charts at the time, Depeche Mode sang 'People are people so why should it be that you and I should get along so awfully,' and this constantly played inside my head.

Sometimes I sang it aloud through gritted teeth.

One Thursday night, when the Personnel Officer had gone home, I received a telephone call from the Head Office wages department. HQ Wages department NEVER called!

I was told that the wages information for that week had not been received, and this would mean that NO overtime payments would be made, NO regular bonuses, etc. Now, I knew that there were A LOT of overtime payments AND A LOT of special bonuses paid out every week, as there were staff who worked constant nightshifts who received regular bonuses.

But it looked like nothing would be paid out...

I looked across the desk and saw all the paperwork still lying there undone.

I'd been so angry and preoccupied with the stupid Manager and his stupid coffee that I hadn't posted the wages paperwork!

These guys were going to string me up.

Panic set in, and I began to feel very unwell. Tingling started in my fingers, loud sobbing noises escaped, and I had a feeling of light-headedness and sickness.

I was going to lose my job.

There was an adjoining door between the Personnel Office and the Store Manager's office, so I tried to keep it locked when I could. But suddenly from that doorway, a head popped round – the Store Manager! That was ALL I needed! If he asked me to get him coffee, I was walking out!

But, to my surprise, I saw a look on his face that I'd never seen before. He looked concerned and asked me what was wrong.

I blubbed everything out through snot and tears and waited for his response.

'Am I fired?' I asked, blowing my nose, and piling the paper tissues up in front of me.

He laughed. 'No, you're not fired,' he said, with a slightly bemused look on his face. 'Right, first things first, let's get you some coffee.'

He left the office and headed for the staff canteen, and I could hear his shiny leather brogues echo along the corridor.

He worked late with me that night, trying to sort out the situation. We would make a note of all the payments to be made and add them to the wage packets manually, then next week when they came through from Head Office we would take them all back again – manually.

It was a huge amount of work, but I did it with his help. And I never forgot to post the paperwork again.

I saw a different side of him that night – a side I'd never imagined he had. A very caring side.

Interestingly, he never asked me to bring him coffee again after that. Instead, he brought me coffees.

People are people.

Chapter 9

Love Train

November 1982:

I caught the rickety old train on the Saturday morning, and it chugged slowly north to Inverness. It was a freezing November morning, and a thick covering of furry white frost glistened on everything, leaving grass and fences all sparkly and velvety.

My stomach lurched with the movement of the train. There was only heating in one carriage – the buffet carriage – so I was allowed to sit there for the full four-hour journey, as long as I had food or drink in front of me.

I cradled a coffee cup in my hands and stared at my Mars bar. I didn't feel much like eating.

The trauma of the past few weeks still played a part in my mind through flashbacks and visions. Sometimes I'd look from the bus window into a car below and see the people inside all smashed up and blood splattered on the car windows. Then I'd blink and it was gone. Then there were the nightmares of the spinning and spinning before I woke up.

My tall guy had suffered a crushed leg and a broken hand, and it would be some time until he could return home. He had been in 'traction' for a couple of weeks, but the previous day there had been an operation which lasted five hours. I mean, why would it last five hours? What could they be doing for five hours?

On the day of the crash, a doctor had spoken to me and said there was significant damage and he would **try** and save the leg. Try and save the leg!

Maybe they hadn't managed to save it. Maybe they'd had to amputate.

How would he manage? How would **I** manage if my boyfriend was an amputee. I had always been extremely squeamish with blood, etc.

I had a long time to think about this on the train journey, and how things might pan out.

The journey involved a four-hour train ride, then the train sat in Inverness for two hours – during which time I could visit the hospital –then I'd take a taxi back to the train station for the four-hour journey back home.

Two hours was a long time to visit if you were throwing up. Would I be able to face this visit? Would I be able to face a life with an amputee? I was very shaky and nervous. As the train wound its way north, nearer and nearer to my destination, I became more and more anxious.

Two drunk guys got on the train at Aviemore. They were very loud, and very happy, chuckling away to each other in a strong accent that I couldn't quite recognise. They lit up cigarettes.

'Du want a fag, hen?'

'Yes, please,' I replied, surprising myself.

It smelled good; it smelled like my dad. It tasted good, too. Hot, glowing, warming, comforting me.

'Where ye off to, hen?' they asked.

I told them the story – the accident, the leg, the operation, and how I was feeling. It's amazing how a chat over a cigarette can bring people together. It felt good to offload onto these strangers.

At Inverness, they hugged me and wished me well. They offered me another cigarette.

'No thanks,' I told them. 'I don't smoke.'

On the night of the crash, I had been stranded in Inverness with nowhere to stay. A tall, blond woman came and spoke to me at the hospital and offered me a bed for the night. She and her husband had been there after her mother-in-law had suffered a fall, and but for a twist of fate we would never have met.

She had bright, sparkly blue eyes and a kind face, and she looked tall and elegant, 'angel-like' in what seemed like a horrible nightmare.

I stayed with these guardian angels for a whole week, and they looked after me and fed me, making me welcome in their beautiful home high up on a hill.

I'd never seen a house like it. I'd never seen a house with a velvet-covered 'chaise-longue'. There were horses and donkeys in the fields, and a very aggressive goose called Charlie, who acted as guard dog. I had to admit I was scared of Charlie.

After my train journey I discovered that my tall guy had managed to hold onto that leg, and he made a slow recovery in the hospital in Inverness over many weeks. During that time our guardian angels visited him, and we forged a new friendship born out of tragedy.

I would watch the autumn change into winter as I waited for the train every Saturday, feeling the icy cold nipping at my fingers and toes.

The real wrench came when he was sent home to his parents' house and couldn't return home to the flat in Fife to recover from his injuries. He would have to go home to Caithness, and it was too far for me to travel.

In the days before mobile phones or iPads, we were forced to resort to writing letters. So, we would write every day to each other –sometimes two or three letters every day, if we had time. I didn't even have a phone in my flat, so we would make arrangements to talk on a Sunday night when I was at my mum's house.

As Christmas approached, we were both very sad. We wanted to be together, but it all seemed so hopeless.

However, his mum and dad obviously saw how unhappy he was, and they bought him a flight south for Christmas. He was coming home to be with me for the holidays. He would take a flight from Wick to Edinburgh, then his sister would meet him there and get him on a train to Fife.

I took a last look in the hall mirror before I left to meet him at the train station. My face was pale and thin, but the infections had healed well, and it didn't look like there was any scarring. I had been lucky.

Chocolate and sweets had been the last thing on my mind recently, but I could see that was to my advantage now, as the little pink dress sat perfectly on my hips. It felt good.

Butterflies fluttered in my stomach as I waited on the platform for the 14.14 from Edinburgh Waverley. Excitement turned to apprehension, and I wondered if we would still feel the same about each other after all these months apart.

My new contact lenses had changed my life dramatically, and I could see everything so much better. I could read the train timetables on the walls of the platform, and I could read the time on the old clock hanging above the waiting room. I could see every blade of grass and every petal on a flower. It was a whole new world.

The old blue train chugged slowly into the station, and I scanned the faces, desperately looking for my tall guy.

At the end of the platform, I could see his sister holding the carriage door open, and then I saw him. Slowly and awkwardly, he managed to get down from the train and make his way along the platform with crutches – one under each arm. Like a child walking for the first time, concentration was etched on his face and beads of sweat trickled down his thin, grey face.

His mum had been very clever with the sewing machine and attached Velcro to his jeans to make room for the heavy plaster cast, which stretched from the hip right down to his toes, with a hinge at the knee.

This was the man who had saved my face from the impact of the crash with his bare hand.

We stood hugging then, my head buried in his strong, broad chest, the crutches holding us both up. And I could see everything clearly.

The pattern of my life was clear and sharp stretched out in front of me. Our lives may have changed that black Monday in October 1982, and they would possibly never quite be the same again. But for that twist of fate on the grassy verge just south of Inverness, we might not have found our love for each other.

PART TWO

'From every wound there is a scar, and every scar tells a story. A story that says "I survived".'

Craig Scott

Chapter 10

Happy Ever After

Is there such a thing as 'happy ever after'? There is in the films. Mostly, by the end of the film, everything has been resolved – all the conflict, etc – and we're led to believe that the handsome couple will go on to live happily ever after.

But real life doesn't work like that, does it?

In real life, the conflict goes on. There are always troubles to overcome and conflict to sort out – some not so easily.

We moved to this old sandstone house in 1988, and we loved its character. With its solemn, old, tanned face, it was like a kindly old gentleman who would look after us. Supported on either side, standing firm in a row, like soldiers straight and tall, joined to each other for better or worse, richer or poorer.

The walls were silent at first. There were older people living on either side of us, and there was never a sound heard through the thick, old, sandstone walls.

After the sweet old lady, who lived on one side, left to be looked after in a care home, her house next door became very sad.

Three long years the house stood empty, the grass grew up, trees and foliage grew up over the windows and doors. The sad old house was deserted and forgotten, and local children called it 'the haunted house'. None would dare to open the squeaky, old gate.

Eventually, the empty house went up for sale in the summer of 1994, and it went to auction at a very low price because it was in such bad repair.

For weeks the viewings went on. Hundreds of people came to look at the house, some with children, some without. And we waited patiently to meet our new neighbours.

Months went by.

A shiny black BMW with tinted windows was seen several times, parked on the double yellow lines.

Then at last work started and the poor old house was ripped apart, plaster ripped off every wall and taken away in bags, roof taken off and the windows removed, leaving it like a skull picked clean by the vultures.

Day and night workmen came and went. Huge sheets of polythene protecting the house from the elements kept us awake each night, cracking in the wind like thunder.

On the yellow lines sat the shiny black BMW, and now a convertible in blood red.

His and hers. Perfect.

From the BMW emerged a dark-haired young man, suntanned, wearing dark glasses. The female was small and blonde.

As time rolled on, we watched the house take shape and it became the most beautiful house in the street, with new windows and doors, and beautiful curtains with frills and ties at every window.

How did they finance such expenses? If truth be told, we were envious. We were both working, and working hard, but we couldn't afford these luxuries.

What would it be like to change places with them, we wondered, even for a day?

The building work went on and on, and it became a problem trying to get our car parked. BMW guy had police cones placed right along the road. Did he think he'd bought the whole street?

The workmen were everywhere, messy, cheeky – entering our garden and leaving more mess.
Now and again a big red Mercedes would crawl up the lane at the back of the houses, and three or four 'gangster types' would enter the back of the house from the rear. Their heads were always down, never looking up.
One day BMW guy almost caused a crash in the front street. I was driving up, and he pulled out abruptly, his flashy BMW with the tinted windows stretched right across the road in three-point-turn mode.
I was driving my friend's old Polo, taking the children to nursery, so I had three little ones in the back of the car.
I rammed on the brakes, and a red mist came down over my eyes...
From inside his flashy motor, he pressed a button, and his window slid down automatically as he raised a hand by way of apology..
Inside the old Polo, I fought with the window handle and spun it round in anger. 'YOU BLOODY IDIOT!' I bellowed at him, shaking, raging.
From inside his shiny motor, he lifted his glasses, and for the first time I could see his emerald green eyes. Then he replaced the glasses and drove off.
I confronted him in the back garden one day when his builders were in our garden leaving their mess. No permission, no apology.
'WHAT'S WRONG WITH YOU PEOPLE?' he roared at me. 'I'm just trying to make my house nice.'
A real argument then ensued, and he was given a few 'home truths'. We shouted at each other over the garden fence, and I became aware of the workmen from the builder's yard across the street all standing, arms folded, a concrete presence waiting to see the outcome of this situation.

To my surprise, he apologised. He said he was sorry for the mess and the inconvenience.

But he required an apology for my outburst in the front street when I called him ‘a bloody idiot’. He was not at all happy about that.

Peace was resumed, on the outside at least. But that night, the walls screamed. It went on and on. Knocks and bangs and much screaming. The walls roared in pain as I covered my ears.

We didn’t see much of the female in the two years they lived there, but I did see her once in the ice-cream shop, buying milk. She tried to turn away quickly so I couldn’t see her battered and bruised face.

And from then on, I didn’t envy this woman with the shiny red car or the beautiful curtains with the frills and the ties. She deserved it all, and more.

It was a freezing December morning the last time the walls spoke. There was much crashing and banging, and then silence.

From behind our bedroom curtains, we watched the beautiful shiny BMW being loaded onto the back of a tow truck. He’ll certainly have no need for that now, where he’s gone.

The walls are silent again.

But between the tough old bricks and thick old cement, the memories live on.

Chapter 11

We Are Family

2003:

Back in school, I was settling in and becoming more competent at my job. With a lot of support from colleagues and management, I was getting there.

Another new woman had started around the same time as me, and we became quite close, sharing lunchtimes together and chatting about our home life as she lived in my area.

One Friday she said her husband was coming to collect her. She said she would phone him and ask if he could take me home too, as we didn't live far from each other, and it would save me time waiting on a bus.

She would need to 'ask' him, which I found a bit strange. If it was my husband, I would just say, 'This is my friend, we're taking her home.'

Then before we got in the car, she took me aside and said quietly, 'If he asks if you were at my house last Saturday, you need to say yes!'

Even stranger, there was something in her voice I detected. It was fear.

I thought about her all weekend. I'd lived in fear for years, but I got out. I was lucky. It seemed this woman wasn't so lucky.

I decided I'd ask her about it after the weekend.

When I got a chance to speak to her on the Monday, she admitted that she wasn't allowed to see her sisters, and she had invited them round the previous weekend when her husband was away. But he had called her and heard women talking in the background so she had said it was friends from work.

I needed to ask the question. 'Has he ever lifted his hands to you?'

She didn't answer.

I repeated, 'Can you tell me he has never lifted his hands to you?'

She didn't answer, but the look on her face told me everything I needed to know.

After that, I watched her daily and thought, there but for the grace of God go I...

She became very friendly with one of the male teachers, and I often heard them laughing together. It was good to hear her laughter, especially since she didn't seem to have a happy home life.

One day, a pupil commented to a member of staff, 'Teachers in the laundry cupboard making sweet, swweett love.' And he made kissing noises on the back of his hand and laughed as he swaggered down the corridor.

No one believed him.

My birthday arrived, and my new friend said she had a birthday gift for me.

How lovely.

To be here doing this job that I had thought completely beyond me and unmanageable for someone like me, felt so good. And I was managing to gain respect, even with the most challenging of pupils, non-verbal pupils, complex pupils.

How wonderful it was to get a word out of the pupils who were non-verbal. One pupil just said my name over and over, but it really touched me.

Another pupil who was non-verbal spoke one day out of the blue. He looked straight at me and declared, 'You're craazzzyyyyy!'

Everyone laughed, and a male member of staff said, 'Aye, he's got you sussed, hen.'

I was part of the team. Accepted. And it meant a lot to me.

Out in the playground, I was alone on duty with the boys playing football one day at lunchtime. They played rough, and God forbid I might need to break up a fight.

The ball kept going over the high wall onto the road, and the boys were itching to go out of the school and get it. I made sure I retrieved it, but after the second time I warned them that if the ball went over the wall one more time I was taking it away.

A chorus of 'Aw, Miss, no, please no…'

As I warned them, I could hear the Headmaster's words in my ears, 'Be consistent, be fair.'

Of course, the ball **did** go over the wall again, and a voice came from deep within me, a voice I didn't recognise as my own, and I ROARED, 'RIGHT, THAT'S IT. I WARNED YOU. I'M TAKING THE BALL.'

I marched down the stairs with authority and took the ball amid the chorus of

'Aw, Miss. Aw, Miss, no.'

From behind me the janitor appeared and asked, 'who was that? Who shouted?'

I said, 'It was me.'

'Well done, wee one,' he said. 'I didny think ye had it in ye.'

One day, a boy came close to tell me something confidential.

'Miss, can you keep a secret?'

'Well, not really,' I told him. 'Depends what it is.'

'Well, it's Sharon. She's got pills in her schoolbag. She says her dad gave her them, and she's giving them to people.'
'Oh no, I don't know if I can keep that a secret, sorry. Are you sure?' I asked, as this had never happened before.
There was no other staff around, as they were covering other playgrounds.
Maybe the boy was wrong, I thought. I decided to ask Sharon.
I called her over.
'Sharon, one of the boys says you've got pills in your bag that your dad gave you. He says you're giving them to people. Is that right?'
Her eyes grew wide, her mouth opened and she gasped, 'No way, Miss! NO WAY! My Dad would NEVER do that!'
'Ok, good, good. Glad to hear it.' I started to relax, my shoulders dropping again. Phew, thank goodness for that.
'It was my uncle that gave me them,' she announced. 'My dad would NEVER do that!'

So, my birthday came around and my new friend didn't come into work.
We had already exchanged mobile phone numbers, but there was no message, no call. She didn't turn up for work, and she didn't report in sick.
I had a very bad feeling in the pit of my stomach. Oh my God, what if she was hurt? Or what if it was **worse?** Maybe I'd simply been watching too many crime dramas!
I also had her landline number, so I called the house. Her husband answered, but he wasn't giving much away.
'No, she wasn't in work today.'

'No, she won't be in tomorrow either.'

And no, I couldn't speak to her.

I was very concerned now, so I called my line manager at home and told her my concerns.

She was a very 'upbeat' kind of woman. 'Oh, don't worry,' she said, 'I'm sure she's fine, and she'll be in in the morning.'

But that's not what my gut was telling me. My gut was screaming at me: 'This is bad... very bad.'

The next morning, I was waiting at the bus stop when my mobile rang. I saw it was my new friend calling. Phew! Maybe I had been worrying about nothing after all.

I answered with a cheery, 'So, where were you yesterday, ya big skiver?'

But it wasn't my friend on the other end; it was a male voice.

'Where are you?' he asked. 'I'm coming to get you. There's a few questions I need to ask you.'

Well, my internal panic button was well and truly pressed and kept on pressing!

'I'm at the bus stop, waiting on my bus,' I said shakily.

'Right, I'm coming to get you,' he said. 'Wait right there.'

'Em, em, my bus is just coming,' I lied.

'Right, I'll be waiting for you at the school.' He hung up.

Oh shit! What was I going to do? Who could I phone at the school to help me?

My legs shook and my heart was racing. Why did he want me?

I had time to think about it on the bus.

Scarlett had given me her mobile number. She knew everything and everyone, and she'd been trying really hard to befriend me recently. So it was worth a try.

I rang her mobile. She picked up. And I told her what had happened.

'Right, I'll see you at the school,' she said. 'Don't worry about a thing.'

Easy for her to say!

As I reached the school, the crazy husband was waiting at the school in his flashy Mercedes. The tinted window slid down, and he told me to get in the car without looking at me – almost 'gangster-like'.

'Em, I need to get to work,' I stumbled shakily.

He was adamant. 'GET IN THE CAR!'

I just kept saying I needed to get to work, but I was shaking and on the verge of tears.

'I demand to know who my wife is having an affair with!'

'What?' I gasped. 'She isn't having an affair with anyone!'

By this time, he was out of the car, and his face was very close to my face. I could smell his expensive aftershave as he towered over me.

Something caught my eye then, and as I looked over at the old school building I could see a row of faces staring out, watching through the cracked old glass.

Two tall figures stood at the school gate, arms folded, standing firm, making their presence known.

The Headmaster and the Janitor.

I ran across the street, tears blinding me by this time, and the Headmaster called over to the crazy husband to move his car or he would call the Police.

The Headmaster asked me softly if I was ok as I ran past him, and told me to go into his room.

There, I sat with my Line Manager and the Deputy Head. I was quite hysterical by that time. This man knew where I lived, as he'd dropped me off at my house.

What if he came to my house?

I no longer felt safe.

We sat in silence until the Headmaster came in, closed the door, and paced back and forward in front of me, asking what had happened, looking very uneasy and uncomfortable as I spoke and relayed the story.

'I'm not entirely sure how best to handle this,' he said.

It wasn't exactly a situation that would be in any of the Head Teacher's guidance books. (How to be a Head Teacher; Volume 6 – Chapter 9, paragraph 12 – 'How to tackle an angry husband when a staff member is having an affair at work'.)

He probably didn't know my home situation at that point and clearly felt very protective towards me.

'Right, here's my house number,' he said eventually, passing me a small Post-It slip. 'You call me anytime, day or night, if you have any problems with that man again.'

As I came out of the Headmaster's room, all the other Support Staff were waiting in the corridor. They all hugged me like family.

Even Scarlett.

She said, 'We were so worried about you. We thought he was gonna kidnap you, for God's sake.'

Scarlett took it upon herself to look after me from then on. She called me at home every night, asking me how my day went, and always seemed to know everything that was going on in the school.

Chapter 12

Tree of Life

The job in the school wasn't easy, and it came with many challenges, but I'd never worked in an environment like this where staff worked so closely together. We really **did** have each other's backs, and I felt supported by my colleagues and Management.

I had loved working in the supermarket and still keep in touch with friends from the 70s and 80s that I worked with.

But this was different.

In-service days were always good. We had interesting days with the Headmaster and the Management Team.

At a two day in-service seminar and overnight stay in a hotel by the sea, a great deal of alcohol was consumed, and some staff slept through the second day meetings!

On one occasion we were instructed to draw a tree. Just draw a tree.

As staff, as grown-ups, draw a tree. There was plenty of laughter and shenanigans, but it was a specific exercise that we didn't know would be studied and analysed.

Some drew tiny trees; some drew their trees too big and didn't leave enough room for growth or fruits. Some had no roots; some had huge roots.

I had huge solid roots on my tree with fruit and blossom, but I didn't leave enough room for any growth.

After we'd all laughed and finished our drawings, the Headmaster explained the significance of the tree. And I was fascinated.

The roots were symbolic of our family roots and how strong and stable they were. The fruits and blossom were significant of personal imagination and ideas. And the size of the tree and where it was placed on the page was significant of where you were in your life: centre page meant right in the moment; too much to the left meant too much in the past; and too much to the right meant you were storming ahead.

My tree was too far up the page, so I hadn't left enough room for growth.

The exercise really spoke to me, and it's something I've never forgotten.

As we all walked round the room checking out each other's trees, I will never forget my male colleague's effort. It loomed large and black in the middle of the page, and it was covered in big spiky thorns – all over it. It was shocking and incredibly sad. I could have cried.

He was troubled, for sure, but there it was in black and white for everyone to see. It was a sign, and we should have known then what was to come.

One year, a regional in-service day was planned, where teaching staff were invited to the local mainstream school to discuss how Education staff could improve attainment in schools.

The invite was for **teachers only**. No Support Staff were invited. We were expected to stay in our local schools and clean out cupboards, no doubt!

The Headmaster replied to the invite to say his Support Staff were **a big part** of his school team, and unless his Support Staff were invited to come along then **none** of his staff would be attending. As a result, we were **all** invited.

It was in the school which my youngest daughter attended, and I was actually a bit nervous.

This school had **not** been our preferred option for our daughters, and timing was bad that year as the Head of Education had decided that local schools should be for local children, and there was a big push on parents **not** submitting 'placing requests' for other schools.

Lots of parents still submitted placing requests, but they were mostly refused.

So, our daughter found herself at the local high school – unlike her older sister, who was at a different high school.

As this was second time around for us, we had something to gauge the school by, and I would not remain silent if I thought things weren't right.

S1 parents' night came around, and my daughter came home with a message from teaching staff. She said some teachers were pulling names out of a hat for appointment times. Some teachers were complaining that there were too many pupils in the classes, and they would not be able to see **all** parents, so they had come up with a system whereby they would prioritise the neediest of pupils.

In my daughter's words, 'only the badly behaved pupils or the really clever pupil's parents'. Which would not be her, she'd decided.

It reminded me of my own school days…

'Are you sure she's in this class? She's obviously not a troublemaker or one of the top pupils, or we would know her.'

I would not remain quiet.

I had joined the Parent Council and I'd worked hard building relationships with the management team (or so I thought.) I had started a 'numbers club' to raise funds for the school and wanted this to be a success. I wanted to help my daughter, and I wanted to help the school.

However, I clearly remember the evening that I raised this concern about appointments for parents' night, and also the fact my daughter didn't seem to get any homework.

It was a Parent Council meeting, and there were a large number of parents in attendance as well as the Head Teacher and Deputy from the mainstream school.

The Head Teacher's 'hackles' were almost visible at my questions. She was not at all happy with me, and as she leaned forward in her seat so she could see me better, she answered, 'Mark my words, your daughter will have homework from now on!!'

I replied that I would hope it wouldn't just be **my daughter** with homework, as other parents had agreed with me that evening.

The next day my daughter came home from school and asked, 'Mum, did you say something about homework last night at the meeting?'

'Why?' I asked sheepishly.

'Well, it's just that every class I was in today the teacher announced that a parent had requested homework for our class.'

I resigned from the Parent Council after that. There's a time to fight, and a time to protect others.

So, as the regional in-service day approached, I wasn't exactly looking forward to this event.

We were split into small groups of perhaps ten people on the day, and the first workshop was led by our daughter's English teacher. This was a woman who had put our daughter out of her English class and rejected our requests for a 'credit' exam paper.

I'd had a call from the Deputy Head the day before the Standard Exam to say that our daughter would **not** be expected to pass the 'credit' paper and so a 'foundation' English exam paper had been issued.

I complained loudly and bitterly and made it clear that we wanted our daughter to sit the 'credit' paper if she was to have a chance of getting into University.

'She won't pass,' the Deputy Head assured me.

'I WANT HER TO SIT THE PAPER!' I announced firmly.

'It costs money to order another exam paper at this short notice,' I was told.

The whole experience of this school at this point left me with a very bad taste in my mouth.

So here I was as an adult, a parent, facing this woman who had made such a judgement of our daughter and who had such influence over her future. I'd never actually met her, so I don't think she knew who I was, but I knew her.

The group took it in turns to speak and come up with new ideas, new suggestions of how we could improve attainment and improve schools.

'Brainstorming'.

Each person took a turn.

I was very nervous, but the Headmaster had made it clear to us that he'd had to fight to get us at this meeting. 'So, speak up,' he'd said. 'Don't just sit there and say nothing. You are valuable.'

I spoke quietly and shakily and made the point that more School Support staff would raise standards and help kids learn.

We saw a different side of the pupils. We saw them come in in the morning without a schoolbag when their dad had been drunk and violent over the weekend and they'd had to stay at Gran's, so they had no uniform and no schoolbag.

We saw them come in looking grubby and dishevelled, and we knew their dad had been arrested or their mum sectioned.

We saw things that the teachers didn't see. We got the chance to **really** speak to the kids in a way way that a teacher didn't have time to do, and to build a relationship with them. Perhaps raise a concern. Help them 1:1.

The English teacher was writing notes, but she didn't even seem to be listening.

When I had finished, she looked up and with a very condescending, bland voice said, 'Yes, yes, very good. Let's move on.'

I recognised the woman sitting next to me. I think she was a Deputy Head in a primary school. But I will forever be grateful to her when she took her turn.

'I would like to agree with this lady on my right,' she said, 'and the comments she made about School Support staff. And I think we should spend a bit of time discussing this.'

Our younger daughter is creative and talented and was extremely lucky to have wonderful, supportive staff in the Art Department who saw her talent and encouraged her above and beyond their regular duties. But she also needed that English pass to get into Art School. Without it, her path was going to be very different.

We pushed for the 'credit' paper, and she sat the exam. But was the English teacher right to refuse our daughter the exam paper? Were we wrong to insist that she sit the 'credit' paper? Were we putting additional pressure on our daughter?

She had additional help from the English teacher in my school, who gave her extra tuition.

'You've done the right thing,' she assured us. 'She **is** going to pass!'

But still I was unsure.

We were all very nervous when the exam results came that sunny August morning. Both my daughters and I all held our breath as the envelope was ripped open.

A PASS!
A REALY GOOD PASS – not just scraped through.
The three of us danced around the room that morning, hugging and crying and laughing, all at the same time. A seed was planted that day – a seed that would grow and blossom and reach for the sky.

Chapter 13

Bridge Over Troubled Waters

So much happened in that old school with the cracked windows and the leaky doors. Too much to tell. But I can say that there are memories engraved onto each of our hearts following our years there – good and bad, happy and sad. And lifetime friendships forged. Staff in-service days; drunken nights (yes, I learned to drink – only not very well, and staff would draw straws about who would be taking me home before the end of the night); staff Christmas shopping trips to Edinburgh, Germany, Poland, and Madrid; residential trips with pupils.

A local Reachout 'posse' was sent to the school, with a view to starting a religious group in the school. With my church connections, I was approached.

It was something I wanted to be involved in, but I couldn't do it on my own. I would need someone to lead the group, as my religious knowledge was patchy for sure.

I had attended church with my gran when I was small. But I was a bit scared of all the loud talk from the pulpit about 'hell and damnation', to be honest, and usually sat very close to my gran in church, snuggling into her overly large bosom for safety.

My parents weren't churchgoers, and possibly atheists. But I got something from these church visits with my gran, and I learned to pray.

I prayed when I was worried about things. Things a five-year-old might worry about, like...

I didn't know how to do my homework, or my scary teacher might shout at me if I got the answers wrong.

I prayed that I wouldn't get into trouble in class for using 'the wrong hand'.

I discovered that when I prayed about my worries, then somehow or other they worked out. My prayers seemed to be answered.

I learned to trust this God who listened to me and answered the door when I knocked.

In primary school, I was bullied by another girl. She sat beside me, always hanging onto me in class and in the playground, and kept me for herself. I never got to play with other kids – only this one girl.

She said no-one wanted to play with me, only her.

She actually said some pretty mean stuff to me, but I was very under-confident then and believed everything she said.

All kids have a favourite teacher. And my favourite teacher in primary school came out with some wonderful news to the class one summer morning.

She was going to start a 'Scripture Union' group at lunchtimes every Wednesday, and she would talk about the Bible and we would learn about Jesus. I couldn't believe my ears – such exciting news!

But my bossy friend didn't want to go and said that I shouldn't go either.

I suppose this was a turning point for me: would I stick with my bossy friend and let her continue to bully me?

I might have been about ten years old by then and was starting to stick up for myself. So, I took a deep breath and told her that I **would** be going to the club, whether she liked it or not.

I was making a stand, and it felt good!

Of course she came with me, and as an adult I now understand that it was **her** that no-one wanted to play with, and other kids did start hanging around with me in P7, just before High School.

It was sad, but I gradually understood that it was my bossy friend who didn't have friends and tried to keep me away from others.

With a result of this experience, I knew that a lot of kids didn't go to church and had no religious input in their lives. But I knew the difference it had made to me, and I wanted to share the good news with my kids in this school.

We, as staff, did feel very protective to the kids. We all wanted the best for them – the best they could be.

I asked the Religious Education teacher if she would run the lunchtime group with me. But she laughed and laughed. Give up her lunchtime? NO WAY! It felt hopeless.

Then an angel appeared. Well, actually, to be straight she was an ex-Head Teacher who came into the school to volunteer and teach music.

But she was (and still is) the nearest thing we will ever have to a missionary. Very committed and religious, she was delighted to help and we set up the group together. We voted for a name, and the kids decided on 'The Good News Group'.

The Good News Group ran for years and years and started with a handful of kids, but it got bigger and bigger until there were over 20 pupils coming regularly, and it was manic.

I would be policing the kids while the missionary sang religious songs and played her ukulele, seemingly oblivious to the 'mayhem' round about her.

I could be chasing kids who were running around with scissors, or making stern faces to the kids to stop laughing at her. There were a couple of gigglers who came every week and just laughed and laughed.

But they were there, they were part of my group, and I felt very protective of them.

One of the gigglers came to me one day and took me by surprise when he said that he wouldn't be able to come to my club any more.

I thought he and his pal enjoyed the club, so I asked if something had been said to upset him.

'Well, it's like this,' he said, with a very serious face. 'That Mary is obviously a wee liar! She said she was a virgin, and she had a baby!'

'Em, wait,' I pleaded, 'let's talk about this.'

'Nope,' he said firmly. 'I've made up my mind, Miss. I can't be a part of these lies. I can't come to your club any more. It's final.'

A very gentlemanly young man enquired one day, 'Would God understand if I only came to the club every second week?' He really wanted to play cards with his friends at lunchtime, too. So, we made a deal, and he came every second Monday.

Over the years wonderful teachers did join me and helped me run my club. And at the end of each year, we would reward the kids by taking them on a special outing for lunch and perhaps to the cinema.

One year, we had a trip to the cinema to see the Disney film *Maleficent*. It was really well done and caught me by surprise how emotional it made me feel.

At the end of the film, I had tears in my eyes, and the pupil sitting next to me turned to me and asked, 'You cryin', Miss?'

'No, no not at all. I've just got something in my eye,' I lied.

'Miss cryin',' she reported to my colleague.

There was a boy who was a bit troubled and challenging, but he came EVERY week. He asked lots of questions – some quite inappropriate – but nevertheless he came. And he ate all the sweets the Reachout worker brought.

I told the Reachout worker to stop bringing the sweets, as he was obviously just coming for the sweets! But I'm ashamed to say that the boy continued to come even after all the sweets were withdrawn.

When a residential weekend was mentioned by the Reachout worker, my troubled boy jumped at the chance – like it was his first ever holiday.

I tried to put him off, as I didn't want to go and was concerned about his behaviour on the residential. But he wouldn't be put off, and another very quiet boy put his name down, too.

Their parents would need to drop them off at the pick-up point in Hamilton, but neither of their parents had cars or the wherewithal to get them to Hamilton.

I spoke nicely to my hubby and asked if we could pick these boys up and take them to the bus on the Friday night. So that's what we did.

What I will never forget is the two wee faces in the back of the car that dark November night as we drove over the Bothwell Bridge.

It's a very ordinary bridge, to be honest. There's nothing amazing about it, but my troubled boy's eyes shone brightly and his mouth hung open as we crossed the bridge. And he nudged his friend and said, 'Wow, Ryan, look at all the lights.'

I had to turn away so they wouldn't see the tears in my eyes.

Those boys had the most amazing weekend and talked about it for a long time afterwards.

My troubled boy found comfort in my group and with the Reachout workers, and as time went on he asked how he too could become a leader.

Another residential was mentioned, but this time it would be a joint residential with the mainstream school. It was a pilot event, as it had never been done before – additional support need pupils and mainstream pupils on the same residential.

Three girls came forward from the Good News group and put their names down. But I was worried and decided to go with them. I wanted to protect them and keep them safe and make sure they weren't bullied or laughed at by the mainstream kids.

The Friday night came, and we all crammed into the bus – me, my three wee girls, and a busload of very loud, excited mainstream kids.

How was this going to go? I wondered. Would my girls be laughed at or ignored?

I had gone over all the luggage the girls had to bring – over and over – just in case they forgot something important like medication or something.

There was a list of items they had to remember, but the ASN kids needed help to organise themselves and to remember things.

Some of the parents needed help, too. So, as the girls went in for showers that night, I checked they all had towels, toothpaste, etc.

My three wee girls were totally accepted and included very quickly that night on the bus, as everyone shared sweets and silly jokes.

I felt very proud and emotional to be included in this pilot event and quite overwhelmed at the friendship between the pupils. We really were building bridges between the schools with this kind of event.

When I thought my three wee girls were safely tucked up in bed that night, I could finally relax so I headed off for a shower of my own... only to find that I didn't have a towel. I had forgotten a towel.

From behind me, a cubicle door opened and out came Anna.

'You ok, Miss?' she asked.

Well, I had to admit to her that I had actually forgotten my own towel, after spending days reminded the girls about everything they had to remember.

Anna didn't laugh; she didn't judge.

'My mum put a spare towel in for me, Miss,' she informed me. 'I'll just go get it.'

I felt very humbled. And I had a lovely hot shower then, and dried myself with Anna's brand new, fluffy pink towel.

Now, anyone who does laundry will know that brand-new towels often need to be washed before they are used, or else the fluff will come off.

Inside the shower cubicle, I wiped the steam away from the mirror, and there in front of me stood a small Teletubby lookalike, completely covered in pink fluff from nose to toe!

A laugh caught in my throat and then spread to my eyes, and then leaked out into the air as I laughed and laughed.

From outside the cubicle, a small, quiet voice asked, 'Are you ok, Miss?'

'I am,' I said, through the laughter. And for once I actually was.

I was more than ok.

Chapter 14

Meet Me at Warwick Avenue

March 1983:

So here we were, six months after the car accident, and we'd found a very special relationship together. My tall guy was the most interesting guy I'd ever met. And he made me laugh – a rare trait compared to some of the other guys I'd dated.

I admired his courage. 'Hold my crutches,' he instructed me, as he got into his friend's car to drive for the first time since the accident.

And he was off; we were both off.

His friend needed someone to look after his car and keep it running after he had been caught driving under the influence of alcohol and lost his licence for a year.

One Sunday, we visited my mum, and she confessed to having kept something from me.

She produced a box of letters. Letters that my crazy friend had sent over the past year. One a week, it seemed. In the final letter, he said he wanted to meet me and sort everything out.

He apologised for everything, and there was a rendezvous mentioned in the town the following week.

Mum said she felt safe giving me the letters now as I was happy and settled with my tall guy.

Tall guy stood and rose to his full height. 'I want to meet this guy,' he declared. 'Let's go.'

Well, my legs started shaking again, and I felt physically sick. I certainly didn't want to see him again. And my tall guy had no idea what I'd gone through, and no idea of how this rendezvous made me feel.

He was still walking with crutches, so hardly able for my crazy green-eyed monster who admitted he enjoyed the sight of blood.

Over the next week we agreed we would go to the rendezvous point, but we would sit at the back of the bar in the dim light and see if he turned up.

Tall guy wanted a look at him.

As we sat at the very back of the bar that night in the dim light and watched from afar, we saw my crazy friend enter the bar and sit on a stool right at the front.

His yellow-blond hair lit up under the spotlights. I never was very sure if it was a natural blond. Not many things about him were natural.

My tall guy wasn't going to be intimidated by him and went up to the bar for a second drink. My heart felt as if it had jumped into my mouth, and loud beating came from my chest and through my ears.

Then, as I watched, my tall guy went off to the gents, his long slim legs striding slowly, steadily, with crutches supporting him.

My crazy friend followed behind him.

Those few minutes while they were both out of sight were traumatic and scary, and my mind ran off at speed to the clubbing days when the music would stop and the lights would go up, and there on the dance-floor I'd see my crazy friend smashing someone's face against the floor, often just because he didn't like the look of him. Blood would be splattered across the cold, black dance floor.

If that's what he could do to a complete stranger, what would he be doing to my tall guy right now? I could feel the sweat under my arms and my throat was dry and closing.

Minutes passed, and I became extremely anxious until the gents' door opened and both guys came out, one behind the other, single file, all very civil.

It was to be the last time I ever saw my crazy friend, although he came into my mind often in my nightmares – always the same one. In the dream, I'd be fighting with a door, trying with all my strength to close it and pull the lock, while from the other side he was pushing hard to get in. Sometimes he got in, and then I'd wake up in a really cold sweat. I lived for years in dread that he would ever find out where I lived on the west coast.

2004:

It was a very normal Monday morning when Mum called my new mobile phone. I was on the school bus and we were going to the park for a class outing.

She simply read out an intimation of death in the local newspaper. 'Son, brother, father, grandfather.' No 'dearly loved', no 'sorely missed'. Just date of birth, and date of death. That was it.

My crazy friend had obviously reached rock bottom, and I heard from an old friend that he had taken his own life.

He came. He lived, but there was no love there.

How sad to live a life without love. It's one of the saddest things I've ever heard.

Chapter 15

Love Hurts

Our family in the old school grew in numbers. I was part of a group of staff who mostly worked with the complex learning groups, and we needed new ideas for activities. We were invited into the Headmaster's office to discuss new activities, and we would 'brainstorm' together as a team.

My sister was involved with Riding for the Disabled, so I was able to put this idea forward and get information directly from her.

It proved to be a success, and for many years I took a small group of four pupils every Tuesday to the Riding Centre in Glasgow, together with a lovely staff member who had retired but came back and volunteered in the school each week. We were a great team.

It was wonderful to see these pupils ride and enjoy the activity. And the horses amazed me. They were so tolerant of our kids. It was as if they knew the children had a few difficulties.

One Tuesday, as the team worked to get a boy off the horse and back into his wheelchair, the horse turned his great neck around. And as we slid the boy gently into his chair, the horse laid his great head in the boy's lap and stayed there, allowing the boy to pat his soft hair. There wasn't a dry eye in the place. It was very moving.

On one occasion, a different pupil joined us. He was a pupil who was well known for telling lies, which made us doubt everything he said.

As the school bus trundled its way through Glasgow, there was much excitement and chat from the pupils, and the driver joined in, teasing them about how he would enjoy a McDonalds lunch while they were riding. There was plenty of laughter. Then one boy wanted to talk about his birthday.

'It's on the fifth of August,' he informed me.

'I know,' I said.

I had known this boy's parents for years, even before he was born. So I knew his birthday was on the fifth of August.

Then the girl sitting beside him said the same. 'It's my birthday too on the fifth of August, Miss.'

'It is?' I questioned. 'Really, that's amazing!'

'And it's also my mum's birthday that day and my dad's.'

'What!' I exclaimed.

I may have been gullible, but this was too far-fetched even for me.

The final straw came when the boy who constantly lied butted in, 'Miss, it's my birthday too on the fifth of August.'

Right, I thought to myself, enough is enough! I could feel myself getting annoyed by yet another lie from this boy.

I grabbed my bag from the floor of the bus and swung it hard onto the seat.

'Ok then, Sean, so can I just remind you that I have ALL the permission slips right here in my bag, and I can just look right now and check your birthday!'

'Yes, Miss,' he replied politely.

'So, is there anything you want to say to me before I get your permission slip out?'

'No, Miss.'

I pulled the papers out of my bag in a dramatic fashion, and out of the poly-pocket carriers, and couldn't believe what I was seeing...

ALL three pupils did indeed share the same birthday – they'd all been born on the fifth of August.

It was quite extraordinary, and it turned out the boy had indeed been telling the truth. I felt ashamed for doubting him, but he **did** have previous.

When we reached the Riding Centre, we had a surprise visit from the girl's dad – a lovely, friendly man who stood and chatted with me while the pupils were riding around the indoor arena. I told him about the conversation on the bus that day and he smiled.

'I know,' he said with a laugh. 'What's the chances of that – us all having the same birthday? We couldn't believe it when the baby was born on the same day as our birthdays.'

Back in the school, another new idea was brought in. It was decided that we would have registration first thing in the morning AND last thing before home time. The idea was to catch the kids before they went home, and to discuss any problems/issues so they didn't go home worrying or dwelling on things. It would allow teachers to sort out any issues same day.

It was an excellent plan and worked pretty well – mostly.

However, my registration group was very challenging for me, and I dreaded the last 15 minutes of school with the class I had. It was a 4th year class with some very challenging pupils, including the boy who had laughed at me, and the girl with the pills in her bag.

Fifteen minutes can seem like an eternity when kids are shouting and squabbling and throwing things around the class.

The registration teacher was a lovely lady, so kind. Too kind, and also a bit inappropriate at times.

I joined a maths class she was taking one day and became aware that all these 4th year pupils were using **real** money to count.

'Mrs Fisher,' I interrupted her. 'Sorry, Miss, are you using **real** money for this exercise?'

'Yes,' she admitted, 'the kids seem to get so much more out of it when I use real money.'

'I bet they do,' I said incredulously.

She was such a lovely person, and we would always know when she was in the school –you could follow the line of car keys, sweet wrappers, even perhaps the odd piece of underwear trailing up the corridor towards her room.

I remember one particularly raucous afternoon just before home time. The kids were high as kites and there was no calming them down.

Poor Mrs Fisher had obviously had a hard day, and she stood up at her desk and burst into tears. Then she picked up her handbag and walked out, leaving me ultimately in charge.

My mouth hung open. What should I do? Try to calm the class? Call for help from Management, or another teacher?

Sharon – the only girl in the class of eight boys – jumped up onto her feet.

'RIGHT!' she shouted at the boys. 'Look what you've gone and done now. You've made Mrs Fisher cry! You should be ashamed of yourselves!'

Every boy in the class sat down quietly and immediately listened to Sharon. She was doing a better job than I could hope to do, so I let her get on with it.

After a few minutes, Mrs Fisher did return to the class, by which time Sharon had restored order and made the boys apologise to her.

'Sorry, Missus Fishherrr,' the boys drawled in unison.

In my second year in the old school, I was assigned to a 1st year class, and in particular a pupil in the class who could become challenging.

I commented to the Headmaster one day in the passing, 'What a cutie.'

'Watch him,' he warned me. And he was right.

The boy did indeed become challenging, and I was definitely NOT fit for him. In fact, he ruled the roost for a good while, and it turned out that there was actually only ONE member of staff that the boy would respond to.

This tiny first year boy had me by the hair in the playground, down on the ground, kicking into me. He seemed to have 'super-human' strength and I couldn't manage him.

This called for extraordinary experience and a tough hand.

We called Mrs Smith.

Mrs Smith was a 'take no nonsense' kind of person, but she was fair and kind underneath the exterior of pure steel.

The S1 boy LOVED Mrs Smith. In fact, he actually thought she was his wife and said so on many occasions. He hated Mrs Smith's real husband with a vengeance and would attack him if he got the chance.

I have to admit to 'using' Mrs Smith on many occasions. Like the time when I was assigned to collect him from his house, and he was running around the front garden terrorising his mother with a pool cue.

I shouted, 'GET IN THIS BUS RIGHT NOW OR I WILL BE CALLING MRS SMITH.'

'Awright, awright, I'm coming,' he said nonchalantly. Then he laid down the pool cue and got on the bus like a lamb.

On another occasion I found him in the staff room brandishing a vegetable knife, and there was no-one around for help.

I realised that if I let him see how scared I was, I didn't know how this would end.
'THROW THAT KNIFE DOWN RIGHT THIS MINUTE OR I WILL GET MRS SMITH!' I yelled.
Immediately he dropped the knife on the ground, and I shakily walked him to the Headmaster's room.
He was very challenging indeed and seemed to challenge even the most experienced members of staff.
One day the emergency button rang out, and staff ran to a classroom in the link corridor, which joined the two main parts of the school.
My line manager ran, and I hurried behind her in support. She always said that it wasn't good to have too many staff when dealing with a difficult situation, as it made things escalate, and too many voices in the room was always a bad idea, adding to any confusion that was happening.
So, the situation was that the teacher had called for help as our first-year boy was holding the rest of the class hostage, holding up a gun while shouting and ranting. He was standing on top of a line of desks, and the other pupils were crying and distressed.
The Headmaster was out of the school, so my line manager took the lead, trying to talk the boy down quietly and calmly.
We weren't sure what his demands were; it wasn't clear. Mrs Smith was not in school, though, so that might have been the problem.
One by one we managed to get each pupil out of the room safely, as objects were thrown at us, china mugs crashing off walls.
Eventually it was only my line manager and myself left with him in the room. Still the boy continued to rant at us, holding the gun out.
My line manager spoke slowly and calmly. 'Give me the gun,' she said moving gradually closer and closer to the boy. I was behind her.

'Give me the gun now,' she said very slowly but assertively, talking to him, keeping her eyes on him the whole time. Moving closer. Both of us, side by side.

It was like a scene from a film; a dangerous hostage situation.

Finally, I whispered in my boss's ear, 'You **do** realise it's his hand, don't you?'

She was still taking the situation very seriously.

'It's just his hand, it's not a real gun,' I pointed out the obvious.

The laughter started in her twinkly blue eyes, and then reached her mouth, and she tried to stifle a laugh. But she couldn't hold it. She had the most infectious laugh, and before long we were both doubled over giggling, and the boy was laughing too. He'd forgotten all about his hostage demands, and the situation was defused.

While the S1 pupil loved Mrs Smith, it was a very complicated working relationship and one that needed careful management.

On one occasion I was asked to take him for a walk to a café for a juice. Simple enough, I thought. How difficult could it be?

We walked slowly and chatted about things he wanted to chat about as always – usually Mrs Smith.

We had to walk past the local Woolworths shop before we came to the café. As we passed Woolies (as it was affectionately known), he ran into the shop and grabbed some video games off the shelves, then he made a run for the door like a participant from 'Supermarket Sweep'. Grab and run, just like the TV programme; time was of the essence.

Security guards stopped him before he got out the door, but there was then a situation whereby he was lying on the ground on top of the aforementioned video games, refusing to hand them over.

I had forgotten my mobile phone, so this was a sticky situation.

I tried to negotiate and even used Mrs Smith's name, but to no avail.

Then from across the road I spotted his mum.

'Look, there's Mum,' I tried in desperation. 'Let's go see Mum.'

He jumped up in a flash, and then he was off and running, me sprinting behind, trying to get my hands on him.

Mum was standing outside of the 'Pound' Shop. She kindly gave him 20p to spend in the shop, but my heart sank when he lifted a giant sword off the shelf.

I don't know how much time had passed by this stage, but a search party had been sent out from the school to look for us.

As we finally reached the café and sat down, Mrs Smith appeared.

Everything else paled into insignificance, as the pupil showed off his giant sword to Mrs Smith. He was delighted.

The final moments of that trip have lasted with me for a long time and will probably still be very vivid to Mrs Smith.

As we walked along the street back to the school, past all the residential houses with pretty gardens and neat pot plants at the windows, the boy took his chance. He grabbed Mrs Smith firmly and threw her into a bushy green hedge, jumping on top of her.

The hedge collapsed flat into the garden, and as I looked up I saw an elderly lady at the window.

To this day I can still see the shocked look on that lady's face as she peeked out through the pretty, frilled curtains.

Chapter 16

I'm a Union Man

Good things don't last forever, so they say. And sure enough, although there were many difficult and challenging times in the old school, there was laughter there, strong bonds formed, and much care and respect between staff and pupils.

A petition was raised by local people to stop the new school build. There was passion and a strong fight, but in the end the battle was lost and the new school was built. Our Headmaster retired and a new leader was appointed.

Unfortunately, the new leader led from the back.

On the first day, all the staff had to twist their necks round to see the new leader, who was sitting at the back of the room.

And the new leader continued to lead from the back. Everyone else in front. In the firing line, in the dugout. Taking the hits.

And the hits were numerous.

The new leader was safe in their cosy, warm room with the lights out.

Hits are logged, we were told. Fill in a form. Put it in writing.

So, we filled in the forms... over and over, for two years.

When a member of staff left the school in an ambulance, enough was enough and we decided to go en masse to see our local Union Representatives.

We had been led to believe that all the forms we were completing would be sent to the Health & Safety Executive, through the Union. We were sure they would see our troubles and be able to action some kind of help.

But no-one helped. No-one came.

I remember that evening quite clearly, the look on the Union Reps' faces – their shock and horror at our stories. They clearly had not received ANY forms, so they knew nothing of our troubles.

We raised a grievance. Many staff signed it, and we took our plight to the big glass building with the folk in the suits and the heels. The suits and the heels seemed equally as shocked at our troubles.

We were organised and professional, and we had a timeline with photographic evidence. In the end, we won the grievance and an 'Action Plan' would be put into place.

New guidelines in relation to Health and Safety at work and violence in the workplace would be brought in, and there would be a new company policy, 'Promoting Positive Behaviour'.

But the grievance led to a lot of bad blood.

Bad blood ran in the corridors.

At night my nightmares were strong. A tiger was chasing me wherever I went, beautiful, striped, and terrifying. I tried to shield the children in my nightmares, and I did my best, but the tiger always got me in the end.

Then I had an epiphany.

I would become Union Steward. I would act on behalf of the staff to stop the hits, to stop the bad blood. Take a stand.

Mrs Smith would join me – we would take on the role jointly. I had never felt more strongly about anything.

There were barriers we had to overcome, to get permission for training, for example. But I felt supported by my Union colleagues, felt safe. Colleagues in the school came to me daily with Health & Safety issues, and I managed to get permission to attend a Health and Safety meeting at the Union.

Actually, this wasn't the first time I'd had an epiphany. It had happened once before.

There had been an accident in my church, and luckily no-one was badly hurt.

But I was on my 'high horse', writing letters and raising concerns about equipment. My concerns, though, fell on deaf ears. Nothing changed. The equipment was not replaced, and I was taken aside and told to stop going on about it.

One night I dreamed that I was trying to lift a huge wooden crate. It was massive, and I couldn't lift it as it was too heavy for me.

In my dream I tried to get round the huge wooden crate, but I couldn't manage it. I tried to lift it, but each time I did I was left with big skelfs of wood in my fingers. In the dream a massive hand lifted me up and carried me away from the crate, and I immediately felt a sense of peace.

I shared my dream with a church friend the following Sunday as we walked to church.

'Well, I think it's obvious what it means,' she said confidently.

'It means there's an obstacle in your life that you can't fix. You need to leave it and walk away from it to get peace.'

That made total sense, and I thought long and hard about it that evening. It wasn't the first time I'd had dreams like this, and I always felt there was a message for me in the dreams.

It was around midnight that night when suddenly a thought dawned on me – well, it didn't just 'dawn' on me, it smacked me right in the face! I felt as if someone had run into the room and smacked me right across the face with a wet fish!

I knew the School Chaplain pretty well by now. and his church was in the next town. I got along well with him, and suddenly it all became clear: I would go to him and ask if I could come along to his church.

I shared this news with my church friend, and she was sad to be losing me as we wouldn't be seeing as much of each other. However, a few months later she told me that she too had experienced a dream out of the blue.

She dreamt that she saw me walking to my new church and I was wearing the most beautiful flowery dress. It made her feel happy to know that I had made the right decision, and she was happy for me.

Back in the new school, I had my lunch and then I set off to get the train to the Union meeting. I wasn't entirely sure what to expect, but I felt strong and vindicated.

On entering the building and showing my ID badge, I was shown upstairs to a very plush, empty boardroom with a very large, grand, polished mahogany table surrounded by around a dozen plush chairs. There were beautiful paintings on the wall and the room smelled of fresh coffee and new carpets. I sat alone in the silence, waiting for others to come, and eventually helped myself to a cup of fresh coffee and a biscuit.

After about 10/15 minutes, a group of men arrived in the room chatting and laughing, then stared over at me. No-one said anything to me. There were no other females in the room, and I felt I was sticking out like the proverbial sore thumb. They weren't quite sure what to do with me.

A smallish, cheery-faced man came in and took his place at the top of the large board table. Then we went around the table, introducing ourselves, and I felt totally out of place.

I was wedged between two very large 'blue meanies' with huge bellies, and their blue shirts were showing the strain. I could imagine a button coming flying off a blue shirt and catching someone in the eye.

Most of the agenda went over my head, and I didn't understand half of the chat about legal documents and the 'nitty gritty' of the fine details in employment contracts. Other discussions involved tea break allowances, formal and informal, and Health & Safety for traffic wardens, school janitors, council plumbers and electricians.

The oversized 'blue meanie' on my right surreptitiously slid over a handful of Union pens and tiny notebooks like I was a child at a grown-ups' dinner party.

On each item in the agenda, I tried to get a comment in: Could I volunteer for workshops, extra training, residential courses?

But each time the small, cheery man shot me down...

'All in good time, lass, all in good time. Wait til your training is finished.'

DRRrrrrrrrrrrrrrr... DRRrrrrrrrrrrr... Got me. I'll just sit here quietly like a good girl.

Then curiosity got the better of the guy sitting across from me. 'Why are you here, lass?'

I started to explain some of the concerns that my colleagues in the school had been raising.

A silence fell.

The small, cheery man wasn't smiling any more. His face was long, and his eyebrows were raised.

'What you saying, lass?'

'No, no, that can't happen. No, no, no.'

His eyes were huge now, and he was staring right at me. I certainly seemed to have his attention.

I finally got the chance to say why I was there and have my say. As I spoke, the small, cheery man laid his forehead on the polished table.

While I continued to speak, he began to knock his head against the table over and over, louder and louder.

'NO! JUST NO! THIS CAN'T HAPPPEN!' he shouted then, and everyone was silent.

'Ok.' Finally, after a long painful silence, he raised his head.

I really didn't know what to expect. I didn't know what he was going to say to me. Had I crossed the line? Had I said too much? Was I about to be chucked out of the Union before I'd even started?

He put both hands over his face, covering it completely, and he was breathing very deeply. Then he took his hands away and I waited, heart pounding, for a response.

'Right, this is what you're gonny do, lass.' He looked very seriously at me. 'Next time ANY of these incidents happen, you are gonny phone me, and I'm gonny come right out to your school.

'You are gonny march round to your Head Teacher's room, knock the door, and say I'm coming out to the school. Is that clear?'

'Even if it's before my training?' I asked, trying to be clear.

'YES!' he replied firmly.

Chapter 17

Leavers' Prom

Some might say that the Leavers' Prom was the highlight of the school year.

There was always lots of excitement and talk about outfits – especially between the girls. Hairstyles, make-up to discuss, and not to forget the nail appointments.

In my day (in the 70s) there was no such thing as a School Prom. But both my girls had them, and I particularly remember the cost. Dress + shoes + hair + nails and accessories. The final cost was certainly in the hundreds of pounds. But the photos were beautiful, and a good time was had by all.

It was exactly the same at the ASN School Prom. Beautiful outfits and a good time had by all.

Some of the pupils, though, needed support to get to the Prom, or support during the evening, and support to get home.

One of the pupils I was working with was the boy who said my name over and over. Quite sweet, you would think, but he might also be hauling at my hair at the same time or swearing at me. He could swear really well and totally in the right context.

We were in Edinburgh one day I remember, and just as we were being lifted onto the school bus by the tail-lift, I saw a lovely friend of mine passing. She worked in the University in Edinburgh, so I shouted her over and introduced her to my pupil.

'Hello, how are you?' she asked him politely.
'Shite,' he responded.
Anyway, my sweary boy would need assistance to get to the Prom. If I offered to help, it would save his mum or his brothers, and I could support him throughout the evening.
During a full-staff meeting, it was commented on that I would be supporting my pupil to and from the Prom, and I would be coming back on the bus.
Everyone thanked me, which I found a bit unsettling. I was supporting my pupil, that's all. No need for thanks.
As the weeks went on, there were more meetings, and I asked who **else** would be supporting the pupils on the school bus on the return journey after the Prom.
No-one answered.
Naively, I'd thought other staff would be on the bus, and I wouldn't be left alone to deal with 17/18-year-old pupils by myself. Pupils who were old enough to drink alcohol.

In the school, there were some great teachers. Some of them had the patience of saints with the pupils, and there were definitely some challenging pupils.
One boy who I had a 'soft spot' for was his own worst enemy, and he managed to get himself into trouble without even trying. I spent my days trying to keep him out of bother while I was assigned to the class.
He obviously suffered with wind in his stomach and constantly got into trouble for passing very loud, smelly farts in classes.
In science class one morning, the teacher was mid-lesson when the boy cocked himself to the side of his stool and let rip the loudest, LONGEST, fart I think I have ever heard.

I don't know what set me off laughing: the absurdity of the situation; the vibrating noise of the fart on the plastic stool; or the very unimpressed look on the science teacher's face. But as I left the room in order to have an unrestrained 'hee haw' laugh, I heard the teacher ask in a very irritated tone, 'Are you quite finished? Can I carry on with my lesson?'

Nevertheless, I was fond of the boy and his 'off the cuff' comments.

One Monday morning he announced, 'That's me, Miss, aff the Vimto. It's no good for you, am having Irn Bru instead.'

He was challenging, and a really cheeky chap.

In English class one day, we had a supply teacher – a very quiet, calm man; a gentleman. He was covering for the English teacher who was off sick, but English was not his subject.

'Right, we'll all take a book from the bookcase and read quietly to ourselves for a short time,' he announced to the class.

My cheeky chap chose a book, and as the teacher slowly walked around checking which book the pupils had chosen, the boy started to read aloud... very loudly.

'BLAH, BLAH, BLAH, BLAH, BLAH, BLAH...'

I'd had enough. I jumped off my seat and snatched the book out of the boy's hand.

'If you can't read properly, then you won't read at all,' I announced with authority.

'Excuse me, Miss,' the very mild-mannered teacher interrupted. 'It does actually say that in the book.'

I opened the book at Chapter One, and sure enough the first paragraph read 'blah, blah, blah, blah, blah, blah...'

I handed the book sheepishly back to the boy.

At the end of term one year, the pupils were given a 'treasure hunt' to follow.

They each had a sheet with letters of the alphabet listed, and they were given the task of going around the school finding an object starting with each letter of the alphabet.

My farty boy finished first. I couldn't believe it.

'So, what did you find for the letter Q,' I enquired.

'That was easy, Miss,' he announced with a huge grin on his face. 'Q-cumber.'

I opened my mouth to correct him, then thought better of it. I had to hand it to him on this occasion, so I'd let him enjoy this moment of glory and accept the prize for first one finished.

In Home Economics, the teacher did not approve of the farting OR the boys yawning.

'THAT'S ALL YOU BOYS EVER DO IN THIS SCHOOL!' she roared on Friday morning, period one. 'YAWN AND PUMP! PUMP AND YAWN!' She was foaming at the mouth.

I was speechless. Never had I wanted to laugh more.

Some of the classes kept **me** on my toes, though, never mind the pupils.

The Information Technology teacher had a very quick sense of humour, and I was forever being caught out even though I tried to keep alert.

He had questions on the whiteboard one day, and the pupils were struggling to answer. I just gave some help – or thought I was helping the kids. So I may have shouted out an answer or two to help the kids.

However, that Thursday during the weekly whole-school assembly, certificates were given out for those who had excelled in class.

To my complete horror and embarrassment, I was called out in front of the whole school and presented with a certificate for 'answering well in IT class'!

The IT teacher stopped me in the corridor at home time one day when he was leaving.

'Got your email,' he said, with a very strange kind of 'mock embarrassed' look on his face.

'But... but I didn't send you an email,' I stuttered.

He smiled and strutted off down the corridor.

I ran into the staff room and fired up a computer. As I logged into my school email, I could see that 'someone' had sent an email to him from my account, saying how much I loved him – even more than my husband.

I never left my email logged in and unattended after that. A lesson learned.

There were many pranks and lots of laughter in the old school, and even in the new school for a time. The pupils loved a laugh, too.

One of the lessons in IT involved programming a small robot called a 'Beebot'.

The kids had to programme the robot from start to finish, round a desktop street plan. It was a robotic bee. The exercise was quite complex, and instructions had to be set turning left, right, or straight on, round the route on the mat to the finish line. It was set up across the desks.

After the kids had all had a turn, the IT teacher turned to me and said it was my turn. Now, programming something like this was not my forte, and I knew I was going to be a complete laughing stock.

I tried to picture the instructions in my head and remember what the kids had done. And I tried to remember what the teacher had told the kids to do.

The kids all crowded round the desk, and they were all rooting for me in such a lovely way.

'Come on, Miss, you can do it.'

'We'll help you.'

'Miss can do this by herself,' the IT teacher announced.

But just as I got started, a knock came to the door and the teacher went to answer it. So his back was facing me as I started to programme the small robot bee.

Each time the robot fell off the track and looking like it would crash onto the floor, a pupil was there catching it quickly and silently replacing it on the track. Not a word was said.

The IT teacher turned back into the class just in time to see my robot reach the finish line, and the class erupted into applause and cheers.

'Did Miss do that all by herself?' he asked with a cheeky glint in his eye.

'Yes,' they all announced in unison – not a smile, not a twitch, deadly serious.

I was so proud of them. Humbled and proud.

So, the night of the Prom arrived, and emotions were running high. The kids were all very excited.

As I was leaving the school, one of the new leaders stopped me in the corridor.

'Here you go.'

I was handed a clipboard with a list of all the pupils going to the Prom, their addresses, and emergency contact numbers. I was 'it'. No-one else was going on the bus that night. I was solely responsible for that busload of pupils, picking them up, and getting them to the Prom and home again safely.

Me, a member of Support Staff.

I felt completely overwhelmed by this new knowledge.

I should have seen it coming, but naively I hadn't.

When I refused to take the clipboard, the new leader was not happy. The new leaders wanted to know what exactly the problem was.

They rose from their seats and followed me out of the door in their flip-flops.

The flip-flops were angry.

I was angry.

I did go to the Prom that night, and I did collect my boy. But I didn't go on the bus. When I arrived in a taxi to get him, his mum and brothers and neighbours all waved him off.

I was overcome with emotion when I saw he was in full Scottish dress – kilt and all. How smart he looked.

Unfortunately, he was a 'three-man' job that night. The soles of his hired shoes were so slippy that he couldn't stand up at all, and he needed supported on all sides.

He was loving the music and constantly wanted up on his feet to dance. So he bounced all night, while two or three members of staff supported him on all sides.

My sweary boy was a boy who needed lots of support. Support in the classroom, support in standing, moving around, and with personal care.

As the night drew to a close, my colleagues and I would take him to the bathroom. Even in the disabled toilet, he bounced, he bounced and bounced. He was loving the School Prom. We'd never seen him like this, and not a swear word had been uttered the whole evening.

As we tried to support with toileting, it became almost impossible, as there seemed to be an intermittent problem with the light. Flicker, flicker, off and on, off and on, bounce, bounce, bounce went our boy. My friend and I began to giggle.

Three staff attempted to help, with great difficulty.

The kilt would need to come off – nothing else for it, as we were struggling in this light.

The bouncing continued... bounce, bounce, bounce... Sweary boy was having the time of his life.

Eventually we were able to help him and then re-attach the kilt. There was a great deal of hilarity, and the more we laughed the more sweary boy laughed and bounced.

We had him holding onto a grab rail in the disabled toilet. Flick, flick went the light, bounce, bounce went our boy.

But as we tried to guide him away from the grab rail, something was wrong. He wasn't coming. He was stuck. What was wrong?

We had only gone and attached the kilt AROUND the grab rail! He COULDN'T MOVE as he was attached to the rail.

Well, that was the final straw. We were on the floor, helpless with laughter. Silent laughing, when there's no noise coming out. Stomach-grabbing, uncontrollable laughing.

And still he bounced.

It was a night we will never forget.

Chapter 18

It's a New Day

2018:

The sun shone into the bedroom though the lime green curtains on that beautiful May morning, and I knew what I had to do. I got up and dressed quickly and headed for the new school campus.

I would sneak in through the mainstream school while the cleaners were in and clear out my locker.

I couldn't go on like this, every day dreading going into work – dreading what the rota would say – usually putting me in three or four different places at the same time.

There were no suits or heels in the new school, only flip-flops.

I had tried to do what was right.

I'd tried to support my colleagues.

I'd tried to communicate with the flip-flops.

But I had failed in all quarters.

Failed to make a difference for my colleagues.

Failed to bring in new guidance – even though an Action Plan was supposedly being drawn up.

Failed, failed, failed...

All I had succeeded in doing was upsetting the flip-flops. And oh boy, they were angry.

There was talk of multiple grievances against me, even talk of a court case for slander. But surely slander could only be brought if the comments/statements I had given were untrue?

And my statements were TRUE.

Nevertheless, it all made for some very bad blood, and there was no going back. I had to get out.

There was no Action Plan.

There was no help coming from the suits and the heels in the tall glass building. They couldn't see us. They couldn't see out of the glass building. But we could see them.

Shame on them.

Chapter 19 – Part One

Full Circle

2001:

The kids grew up quickly. So quickly that I wasn't quite prepared emotionally or financially, and when the last of the childminded kids (the twins) were preparing for school, I found myself at a crossroads where many parents and carers find themselves.

What was I going to do now?

Our oldest daughter was in high school, and our youngest daughter was in Primary 7, preparing for high school.

I'd heard about these new 'Classroom Assistant' jobs in schools and thought about this option, but it was scary. After all these years at home in my own environment, it was going to be a big change going out to work.

I found myself enrolled for an evening class at college. Quite literally, I phoned up to enquire about the class, and the next thing I knew I was giving my name and the receptionist confirmed, 'That's you enrolled.'

As part of the course, I would need to do work experience in a school for a few hours a week. So I was accepted as a student in the local primary school, which my daughter attended.

It was awkward, as I knew a lot of the teaching staff there and many of the children, so I felt uncomfortable using the staffroom.

I volunteered in the school for the first year of my course, then just before the summer holidays I received a phone call from the Head Teacher asking me if I would be interested in a position in the school starting in the August.

The position would be working 1:1 with a pupil as 'Additional Support Needs Assistant'; ASN for short.

I would need to go for an interview.

Well, this was amazing, and I was delighted to be invited to apply.

I got the job.

I was determined I would be professional, and I would not get attached to this child in the same way as I had been attached to the children I'd childminded.

This was different, and a new, professional attitude was called for.

No training was given before I started.

On the first day of this new job, I met the child I would be working with. He had pure white hair and the bluest eyes I had ever seen. He was a truly beautiful child. But he certainly needed support, and I was keen to help him in every way I could.

I would help him put his blazer on; I would help him to do his shoes up; I would help him to open his crisp bag. I could do all of that.

At breaktime on the first day, the Deputy Head shouted, 'STOP! We have spent a whole year teaching him how to do all these things for himself, and you are just un-doing all our good work,' she informed me.

Ooops. I'd thought I was helping.

The Deputy Head was scary, and I was wary of her. I certainly did not want to get on the wrong side of her.

She took me into her office for a chat after breaktime.

'I have never worked with a child with additional needs before,' I confessed.

'Well, we're not exactly experts here either,' she confessed.

This was going to be more challenging than I had anticipated. Even more so, as the boy had yet to acknowledge me or even look at me!

A whole week went by, and he refused to look at me. This was not exactly going the way I had hoped.

The boy who sat across from my pupil did acknowledge me, however, and constantly asked for help.

In week one of the term, I noticed him sitting staring around and not working.

'James, James,' I tried to get his attention. 'You need to do your sums.'

'Aye, I know, Miss,' he said, with a very disinterested face and voice. 'But to be perfectly honest, I canny be arsed.'

James was a sweet boy, and I became very fond of him. He had a kind of raw honesty that I admired and found endearing. He was ready to accept help from me, unlike the child I was supposed to be supporting, who wanted nothing to do with me.

James was slow to do his work but fast in other areas... He stopped dead in his tracks one day in class.

'Miss, are you chewing gum?' he asked me in a very shocked, accusatory tone.

'No, no, not at all,' I lied, and immediately turned away and discarded the chewing gum into the bin.

The class worked on a project about pets, and I told James about our pet rabbit – how I had washed it in a bucket of soapy water and the following day it was found dead in its hutch. He seemed particularly interested in this story.

By the end of the week, I was still struggling to get the attention of the boy I was supposed to be working with. Maybe if I spoke about my girls it might make a difference. I'd found over my years in childminding that often a child would relate better to another child, rather than an adult.

Suddenly the boy turned and stared right into my face. 'YOU... HAVE CHILDREN?' he asked me clearly and intently, as if I was some kind of freakishly weird person that would not be allowed to have children.

'Well yes, I have two girls – one at high school and one at this school.'

'What colour are they?' he asked seriously.

I took this to mean the colour of their hair and went on to describe the one with the blonde hair and blue eyes, and the one with the brown hair and the brown eyes.

He stared at me then for a few minutes and I felt it was a small breakthrough.

After that, any time I mentioned my girls, he would ask, 'Which one, which colour?'

I worked a whole year in that class with a teacher who didn't particularly look comfortable with another adult in the class. There was no conversation. But I always tried to be friendly and professional.

At lunchtime, it was my duty to walk the class up to the dinner hall, and I would stay with them until after they'd eaten.

I led the class from the front, would assist with carrying dinner trays and cutting-up if needed, then I finished for the day.

One day a young teacher took me aside and said that a boy had gone missing from my class the previous day at lunchtime. It turned out he had been left in the class by mistake.

I was horrified. My goodness, was this my fault? Was I about to be disciplined, or fired?

She explained quietly that it was actually the class teacher who was responsible, as she should have made sure everyone left for lunch, but she had attempted to blame me for the misdemeanour.

I knew where I stood from then on.

As the term went on, my hours were increased, and soon I was asked to stay for the full day. That was great – extra wages would come in very handy.
However, I had a bit of a dilemma in that I still did not want to use the staffroom. I felt very uncomfortable.
On one occasion I had been invited to have a cup of coffee in the staffroom and was obviously sitting in one of the teacher's seats. She stood in front of me hovering.
I immediately asked, 'Sorry, am I sitting in your seat?'
'Yes, you are,' she replied.
I jumped up and vacated the seat for her, as I presumed that was what she wanted.
I decided to have a quick word with the Deputy Head.
I made my way to her room feeling like a naughty pupil, butterflies in my stomach.
I knocked the door.

As I entered, she was sitting behind a very large desk, looking scarier than ever. The room was dark, with dusty-looking, old-fashioned curtains at the high windows.
I stuttered, 'I was just wondering, em, from Monday I will be in all day, so I thought I would just have my lunch with the children in the dinner hall, if that's alright?'
'INDEED IT IS NOT,' she bellowed at me, rising to her feet. 'YOU ARE A MEMBER OF STAFF IN THIS SCHOOL, AND AS SUCH YOU WILL USE THE STAFFROOM... AND THEY WILL MAKE YOU WELCOME!'
Goodness, she knew! She knew everything! She read my mind.
Then in a softer voice she said, 'You will not get peace to eat your lunch for the kids asking you to open this, open that, cut their chicken, etc, etc. I will speak to the staff, and you will take your lunch in the staffroom.'

The Deputy definitely had a very strict, severe exterior, but when she smiled there was kindness and a softness there. The smile reached her twinkling blue eyes, and it was kind and genuine.

This job was a very real challenge for me, and my boy saw the world differently from some of the other kids. I had to try and get into that 'mindset' and think like him in order to understand him better.

In class, a girl in his group made a silly joke and looked over at him. My boy did not look impressed, and he did not like anyone looking at him.

'What you looking at, you dumb rabbit?' he exclaimed rudely.

As I looked across the tiny desks, I saw a girl with slightly protruding front teeth and two bunches in her hair, set up high and hanging down the side of each ear. The 'hair do' and the teeth – I could see where the boy was coming from.

Sometimes as adults, we can just take it for granted that children understand things that we understand, but that's not always the case.

We were going on a trip to the park at the end of term. But there was a meltdown by my boy, and he got very upset and angry and was asked to leave the class.

I wasn't sure what was going on, so as we sat outside the classroom – both of us sitting on the tiny school chairs – I went on to talk about the school trip, and what we would do at the park, and how much fun it would be.

'Will you be coming, too?' he asked, staring directly at me then with those big icy blue eyes. I was touched.

I thought about the Deputy, and how professional and efficient she was, and I wanted to be more like her.

I swallowed the emotion and confirmed, 'Absolutely, I will be there right beside you.'

'But where will I sleep?' he asked with a very worried face. 'And what about the bears at the park?'

He clearly thought we were staying at the park all night! Goodness, I hadn't even considered that! And he thought there would be wild animals there, like he saw on the cartoons.

Once I reassured him that we would indeed be coming home after the park, and there definitely **wouldn't** be any bears, I could see him start to relax.

The trip to the park was a success and everyone had a good day, although the whole time my boy kept asking me, 'What about the fun? When does the fun start?'

I didn't really know how to explain what 'fun' is. It's not something you can see or touch or smell. How do we explain what 'fun' is?

I was devastated at the end of term to be told my pupil would be moving on to a different school. I couldn't hide my emotion, and senior management were very kind to me with tea and sympathy.

'Will you be with us next year?' James asked me before the summer holidays.

'Em, no, James.' I tried to hide my emotion. 'I have a new job in a high school.'

On the last day of term, my boy came into class and emptied out a bag of gifts for myself and teaching staff.

I walked with him round to the Deputy's room, and he gave a tiny knock at her door. She opened the door in her usual brusque manner and then saw this small, embarrassed looking pupil holding out a gift for her without a word.

She struggled to find some words, and I caught some real emotion in her face, She thanked the boy, and I saw tears welling up as she turned back into her room.

James also had a gift for me on my last day in the school. He handed me a large card with a drawing on it. I was touched.

'Is this me, James, wearing a long red dress?' I asked, not really knowing what the drawing was.
'Naw, Miss, it's yer deed rabbit with the blood coming out. I drew it myself,'
His face beamed with pride.
To work with children without emotion, empathy, or passion is unnatural, and anyone who **is** able to do that is in the wrong job.

Chapter 19 – Part Two

2018:

So, I find myself offered a job back in the primary school, 17 years on. Right back where I started. Things will have changed – but will it be for the better or worse?

I have changed for sure. I am not that same wee ‘tweenie’ who would stand up and vacate my seat for another member of staff if they were to ‘tower’ over me, staring me out. I am not that same quiet, insecure person who backs off confrontation.

I have grown. Grown in experience and grown in confidence, thanks to my colleagues at the high school, and support from family and friends.

Some staff remain from 2001 – teaching staff and the janitor, and I find myself welcomed back with open arms.

I meet young, enthusiastic Teachers and Support Staff, and immediately feel welcomed.

Day one of the new school year, and there is much bawling. Boys and girls alike.

A tiny blond boy asks me innocently,

‘Are you somebody’s gran?’

‘I am indeed somebody’s gran,’ I reply smiling. ‘But no-one in this school.’

Another boy is having a complete meltdown at the front door and refusing to get dressed. His parents, with a tiny baby in a car seat, are looking very stressed. The parents are wrestling with the boy, trying to get a brand-new white school shirt and school tie on.

I take them aside quietly and distract the boy.

He's red in the face and distressed, as are the parents.

'Would you like to see my school?' I ask him quietly.

He nods.

'So, these school shirts are very harsh and stiff, and not all kids can wear them,' I tell the parents. 'Would you have a soft polo-type shirt at home?'

The father of the boy nods.

'Right, well, we're just going to have a wee look around the school,' I tell him quietly. 'And if you want to nip back home for the polo shirt, we'll be ok here.'

We head into the class quietly and calmly. Other pupils stare at the boy, who is wearing trousers and a white vest, no shirt at this point. But the boy is oblivious.

He hands me a banana as if it is a telephone and says, 'It's for you.'

When a child hands you a banana on the first day of the school term and says, 'It's for you,' you answer it.

I had a nice conversation with Daddy on the banana, and he was soon back at the school with the polo shirt.

This boy was most definitely somewhere on the autistic spectrum, and I had spotted the signs right away. My experience and training from the high school had just 'kicked right in'.

It's sad when you see kids in the playground standing alone or playing alone. And this young boy stood alone in the playground.

Most of the Support Staff I have worked with in schools were amazing and awesome, and they always looked after the kids, trying to keep them safe and happy.

There were occasional disagreements and the occasional fight in the playground, but a primary school fight is much easier to handle than a fight in high school.

And I continued to learn.

After a nasty disagreement in the playground, my new Support Staff friend took two boys aside and said to them, 'Right, well, you better tell me the truth. Who started this?'

The two small boys shuffled about awkwardly from foot to foot.

'Well, I will just go and check the cameras,' she said assertively. 'They will tell me who started this fight.'

The smaller of the two boys owned up. 'it was me, Miss, but he was calling me horrible names, that's why I hit him.'

'There are cameras in the playground?' I asked her quietly afterwards.

'No,' she replied with a wink and a grin.

There are so many personalities and needs in every school. Another Primary 1 boy I was assigned to for a short time had such a scowl on his face. Such an angry boy, and all this at only five years old. Where had it come from?

He told me he hated me, but he seemed to hate everyone. He was unruly and unpredictable, and I was told to keep an eye on him by the class teacher.

On one occasion, he was using scissors to cut out, but I wasn't convinced he was safe or that others were safe as long as he held those scissors.

I tried to help, but he pulled away from me aggressively and shouted, 'GET OFF! I DON'T NEED YOUR HELP! I DON'T LIKE YOU. YOU'RE OLD AND YOU SMELL OF FART!'

Nice!

I'd like to say that had no effect on me. However, it was said with such venom that it really took me by surprise.

I found myself saying, 'Well, other people like me. I've actually got a lot of friends, and they like me.'

I squirted some Avon perfume on myself from my handbag every day after that.

The wasps in the playground were awful that year, and there was mayhem at break times as the kids ran from the wasps trying to get at their snacks.

So, the Head Teacher made the decision that the infant classes would eat their snacks in the classroom until the wasps died off.

The angry munchkin took his snack out of his school bag – a packet of tomato sauce flavoured crisps. My favourite – genuinely.

I told him this and he scowled at me, deep lines running up his forehead.

After a few minutes, the crisp bag was held out, and I looked up to see a different wee face, quite handsome, and he was offering me a crisp.

My heart melted then. He was not born angry – and I wondered what had caused this anger.

'I'm not allowed to see my mum,' he confessed. 'Can you be my mum?'

I stayed at the Primary School for a further three years, working with some very challenging pupils. Some with social needs.

I learned that a 'pinkie-promise' was **not** binding, and that even the youngest of pupils could be very good liars.

I dealt with a pupil with medical and physical needs. Needs that I would never have imagined I could manage. I was surprising myself.

If this child could manage **living with** these needs, then it was the least I could do to support her. Such a brave, strong child, who had been through so much in her short life, she took everything in her stride.

I was helping these kids in the school, getting to know them and building strong relationships, especially with this girl. And we were getting somewhere.

She was learning to drive an electric-powered chair, and she was doing really well. I was proud of her.

One sunny day in June, the class was out in the playground, and as the girl and I took a rest on the little wall at the side of the playground, the class teacher turned around quickly and took a photo of the two of us sitting side by side, my girl laughing heartily. She was happy in this class with her favourite teacher and her lovely friends who cared so much for her. A teacher who made it his life's work to get to know each and every one of his pupils, and to work on their strengths and weaknesses alike.

As he showed me the photo afterwards, I had the weirdest feeling run down my spine. It was almost like a sixth sense. I felt that this might be the last photo of us together. I didn't understand it, but the feeling was strong and undeniable. Was something going to happen to this girl – or to me?

Right through the Covid 19 lockdown, I supported her on a daily basis through Zoom calls and with the support of one of the best teachers I've ever worked with. He treated me with the greatest respect, like an equal.

At last, after more than 20 years supporting children of all abilities in school, here I was really seeing the difference I was making and feeling valued.

But everything was about to change forever.

Chapter 20

Taking the Lead Boots Off

No-one in their right mind would go swimming in lead boots, let's be honest. Unless they had a death wish.

But life can feel like this sometimes; it can feel like you are swimming with lead boots on, being dragged down under the water, and it's a struggle to keep your head above water. A struggle to get through life.

I'm sure many people feel like this a lot of the time. And I have certainly felt like this at times.

I never actually learned to swim properly. I took lessons several times over the years but never mastered it.

After many lessons, my last swimming instructor told me, 'You've kind of found your own individual way of keeping afloat, sort of. It's not pretty, but it seems to work for you.'

I had a fear of the water, and therefore it's almost impossible to relax and let the water hold you. So I knew what the swimming instructor meant.

My technique was to get across the width of the pool as quickly as possible, in one breath, thrashing and flapping, and I could sense others staring at me in the pool.

My mother-in-law had been a swimming instructor and had worked with disabled people over the years.

'I've worked with people with limbs missing,' she announced in frustration one day. 'I've been able to teach them to swim, yet I cannot teach you!'

August 2020:
It was a Monday, I remember. I woke after a restless night coughing – something I'd been doing since the Saturday.
Everyone was talking about this Covid 19 virus, and there had been so many people in hospital, so many deaths.
Never in modern times have we experienced such a thing.
But surely that's what happens to other people.
Not us. Not me.
We'd taken a trip to France to celebrate our grand-daughter's birthday, because the restrictions had been lifted and we had been allowed to travel.
However, as a doctor informed me, 'Just because you **can** travel doesn't mean it's **safe** to travel!'
No-one wore masks in the airport or on the flights. It was as though Covid 19 was a thing of the past – yeah, we're over that now. As if it was gone.
I got up out of bed on the Monday morning and couldn't catch a breath. I literally couldn't catch a breath.
Panic set in, my breathing was shallow, and my head light and dizzy.
I tried to shout to hubby, but nothing came out, no sound.
I slowly made my way downstairs and managed to alert my hubby. He called NHS24 but, of course, **everyone** was calling.
I had inhalers somewhere in the house but hadn't had to use them for a long time, so we took some time to find them. But they were out of date.

My lungs were rattling and wheezing like an old coffee percolator. I was scared.

I was given emergency advice and invited along to a Covid 19 centre. These centres had been set up all over the country, and many were being manned by NHS staff who had come out of retirement to help with the pandemic.

I was met at the door by staff in full protective clothing and told not to touch anything on my way in for consultation with a doctor.

'Hold your hands out straight in front of you, and don't touch anything,' I was instructed.

It felt like I had landed in some strange new universe. It was like something straight out of a sci-fi film.

Everyone will have stories about these dark days when we weren't allowed to travel, and weren't allowed to see our family if they lived outside our region.

It was tough. And I can't imagine what it must have been like for those with parents or relatives in care homes, unable to see them. Or for those living alone.

So, I went through the assessment process that Monday and was allowed home after being prescribed steroids and antibiotics.

But things deteriorated. This virus wasn't done with me yet.

The following week my breathing deteriorated, and while hubby was out one afternoon I began to feel worse and worse. I could hear a horrible rasping noise coming from my lungs. A growling noise. My lungs were growling!

The young doctor at the surgery was wonderful and took immediate action. Paramedics arrived quickly, and I was taken to hospital. But relatives weren't allowed in, so I was alone.

'So, why are you here today?' the nurse in the Emergency Assessment Unit asked, her manner quite off-hand.

'The paramedic thought I had a chest infection,' I replied.

'Oh, is that right? Without an x-ray,' she retorted sarcastically.

Then she listened to my lungs, and she listened to my heart. No words were spoken, and all that could be heard was the wheezing and the growling as I breathed in and out as deeply as I could.

She stopped listening then, and I sensed a shift in her attitude.

'Well, that wee heart of yours is working overtime,' she said, trying to sound jovial. 'It's going like a wee train. Have you ever been admitted because of breathing difficulties before?'

'No,' I replied.

I felt relief. Help was coming.

I was admitted to a ward and spent a week there. I'd never been in hospital before, apart from when our children were born. But in this case I was one of the lucky ones. I got out again.

Many didn't.

However, my lungs have never really been the same since August 2020, and although I returned to work for a few months, things deteriorated more. And then I received a very unwelcome diagnosis the following year.

A rash appeared on my back, and it gradually spread over my whole body, on my face, in my hair, in my mouth.

The young doctor at the 'Out of Hours' surgery at the hospital was very interested.

'We refer to this as "the Christmas Tree Rash",' he informed me. 'I've never actually seen it in real life. Do you mind if I take some photos?' he asked excitedly.

And sure enough, it was the actual shape of a Christmas tree on my back.

Another doctor called it a leukaemia reaction.
I couldn't believe what I was hearing. Leukaemia?
I don't think I will ever forget that lovely young man who spoke to me that evening. A Junior Doctor, he just referred to himself by his first name, and he was so caring.
Would I like to call someone? Could someone come and be with me?
'We're very worried about you,' he said in such a kind, caring way.

I didn't work again.
It was a huge shock, and I was not prepared either emotionally or financially for this enforced retirement. I wouldn't be able to support my girl up until high school as I'd planned.
I felt grief.
Grief for the life I felt I'd lost. Been cheated out of. I felt my life was over. Damn this Covid 19 virus!!
'Stay positive,' people tell you at times like these. But sometimes that's easier said than done.
I have a friend and ex-colleague who set up her own health and wellbeing business, and she practises holistic therapies.
'Mumbo-jumbo,' hubby called it.
That was until he tried the therapies for himself.
Forty years on since the car accident and the leg that was damaged in the car accident was causing problems now.
I took photos of his leg, as it was purple and swollen, and conventional treatments were doing nothing. He was in a lot of pain.
He eventually agreed to go to my friend for some 'mumbo-jumbo' treatments.
He agreed he had nothing to lose, and everything to gain.

He went in with leg and back problems – his whole body crooked and in pain – and came out straight and tall.

In his words, he went in looking like the Leaning Tower of Pisa and came out looking straight and tall like the Scott Monument in Edinburgh. Quite the recommendation!

Within a few hours the whole leg had gone back to the right colour, the swelling had gone down, and for once it looked the same as the other leg.

It was incredible.

This treatment is called Bowen Therapy. It works through gentle movements in specific parts of the body, to muscles, tendons, and ligaments.

Hubby is completely converted now, a regular client of my friend, and is a loyal advocate of the therapy and the therapist.

I made an appointment with my friend for a Reiki session. It was the first time I had been anywhere since my diagnosis and I was nervous and shaky.

Reiki is a wonderful, relaxing holistic therapy which originates from Japan, whereby the therapist may (or may not) lay her hands on the client. And it's supposed to promote relaxation and healing. There are no drugs or needles involved, and it was something I thought I could handle on my first outing since my ill health had spiked.

My friend went on to explain about other treatments she had trained for and what benefits they were supposed to bring.

I would like to think of myself as an open-minded person and a spiritual person, but when she described the Access Bars treatment, I have to admit even I was sceptical.

She went on to explain that it was simply like Reiki for the head, and she would only concentrate on my head. The therapy was supposed to clear the mind of negative thoughts and replace them with positive thoughts. It could also help with Post Traumatic Stress Disorder. She went on to explain that some people found it life-changing – altering their thought processes and emotions, and leading to a happier, fuller life.

So, she told me that there are 32 different points (or bars) in the head which represent different areas of your thoughts and feelings, like emotions, control, creativity, and communication, etc. And by gently touching these points, the therapist can activate and alter feelings connected to these areas.

It was, she said, almost like de-cluttering and re-booting your computer. Getting rid of negative thoughts, and clearing the junk.

'At worst,' she went on to explain, 'it would do nothing.'

Ok, so I had nothing to lose. And it might just help me feel better about my situation, my diagnosis, myself.

There was no doubt I was suffering Post Traumatic Stress disorder from the trauma of the previous year and my ill-health, but also from my years in the High School. I still suffered nightmares about the trauma.

I felt anger for the injustice I suffered.

For myself and others. Others who were also hurt and traumatised. Anger that those in high places had done nothing to help.

My friend in the Union had supported us as much as she could.

And she tried to hold managers accountable, but she reached dead end after dead end.

After I left the High School she still kept in touch with me.

She called me to say that all my colleagues wanted to strike and protest about how I had been treated.
'I had to remind them,' she said with a small chuckle, 'that they wouldn't get paid.'
But that showed me how strongly they felt.
I heard there had been a meeting after I left.
The suits and the heels came from the tall glass building and they brought the new Action Plan.
There was a lot of anger, and the suits and the heels promised a better working environment for the staff.
They gave out copies of the new Action Plan to staff as proof of new beginnings. There would also be new policies to protect staff against violence at work.

But I also heard that the newly printed Action Plans were taken back from staff before the suits and the heels had even reached the car park. Retracted. Confiscated.

So much anger. So much injustice. All rotting away inside my head, festering.

My therapist friend took my head in her hands and just held it. That's all. She held it as I lay flat out on her therapy bed, with the heated blanket underneath and the soft fleecy cover over me, safe and cocooned.
She held it for what seemed like a long time.
My stomach turned over and gurgled loudly for some minutes.
Then she gently moved her hands to either side of my head, and my shoulder became uncomfortable, making loud clicking noises as I stretched my arm out.
This was the shoulder I had injured in a fall more than a year ago.

Then she moved her hands over the top of my head, and immediately I felt completely overcome by emotion.

I cried and cried and sobbed. Grieving. Grieving for this life I'd thought I had, and now it was gone. Everything had changed.

I think my friend cried, too.

Minutes passed, and she just held me.

Then it stopped, and she relaxed her hands.

As I got back into my car that day, I felt something had shifted. Something had changed. I could see and think clearly, and the anger had gone.

I would leave my job on a positive note. I would invite my colleagues past and present, and I would have a leaving party.

It would be a positive step. The first step in the rest of my life.

And I would concentrate on what I **could do** rather than what I **couldn't do**.

The party was wonderful, and colleagues past and present attended. They came, they ate and drank, and as I sat with hubby all we could hear was laughter, everyone laughing and telling stories and celebrating with me.

Celebrating the end of an era. This was exactly what I'd hoped for.

I said a final farewell to the pupils I had been working with in the school, who were very kind in their comments.

'Miss, you don't look old enough to retire.' So sweet.

Out in the playground with my colleagues, 'polo shirt' boy came running over to me.

'Miss, Miss, I've got a friend,' he told me excitedly.

And a small boy with curly black hair and a broad smile stood beside him holding his hand.

'Are you somebody's gran?' the boy asked me innocently.
'I am indeed,' I answered, smiling.

And there it was, I had gone full circle and felt happy that I had done everything I had set out to do.
Hopefully, along the way I have touched a few hearts, positively affected a few lives, and made a difference in some small way to the children and adults I met on my journey.
It has been a struggle at times.
A struggle to be heard.
A struggle to find respect.
But never have I struggled to find love.
Love has always been there – in family, in friends, in colleagues at work, everywhere. In every part of my life.
I wasn't struggling now. Everything **had** changed. But with a new positive mindset and outlook on life, I would make the most of every day I had and do as much as I could.
I would enjoy the sunshine and eat the cake whenever I could.
The lead boots were now well and truly off.

ACKNOWLEDGEMENTS

I would like to relay my thanks to the team at Grosvenor House Publishing co. for their patience with me as ill health took hold of me towards the end of finalising this book and in particular my thanks goes to Melanie Bartle in her patience, guidance and thoughtfulness during a difficult time.

Melanie and the team have guided me step by step in this my first novel.
Helping me to make my dream a reality.

Thanks also to friend and fellow writer Eleanor Gibson for her encouragement and advice during this time.
Please see “Mindfulness The Journcy, Not The Destination.”

www.ingramcontent.com/pod-product-compliance
Ingram Content Group UK Ltd.
Pitfield, Milton Keynes, MK11 3LW, UK
UKHW032155150425
457398UK00001B/3

9 781836 151029